OSHUN

Goddess of Love and Waters

Spirits of the Orishas
Book 5

MONIQUE JOINER SIEDLAK

OSHUN PUBLICATIONS

MONIQUE JOINER SIEDLAK

OSHUN
Goddess of Love and Waters

Spirits of the Orishas Book 5

OSHUN PUBLICATIONS

Book Cover Design by Inkspire Designs

Published by Oshun Publications

9 Old Kings Road Suite 123 #1038; Palm Coast, FL 32137

www.oshunpublications.com

Spirits of the Orishas

Yemaya: Divine Mother of the Ocean

Oya: Goddess of Storms and Transformation

Elegua: Keeper of Crossroads and Destiny

Ogun: Blacksmith of Destiny

Oshun: Goddess of Love and Waters

Obatala: Guardian of Truth, Justice, and Divine Vision

Shango: The Warrior King of Thunder and Fire

WANT TO BE FIRST TO KNOW?!

SIGN UP FOR MY NEWSLETTER TO RECEIVE NEW RELEASE UPDATES & SPECIALS!

mojosiedlak.com/newsletter-signup

Contents

INTRODUCTION
THE FLOW OF LOVE

There are moments in life when we long for something more, more joy, more connection, more beauty. We search for meaning in love, strength in difficult times, and peace when everything feels overwhelming. For many people, the answer to that search comes in the form of a spirit who has walked with humanity for centuries. Her name is Oshun.

Oshun is not just a figure from the past. She is a living presence, a guiding energy, and a source of comfort and inspiration for countless people around the world. Whether through prayer, ritual, art, or simply living with intention, many have come to know Oshun as the orisha of love, beauty, fertility, and sweet waters. She brings a sense of flow, of movement and balance, to the human experience. She helps us open our hearts, listen to our intuition, and walk gently through the world with grace.

This book is a journey into that flow.

What Is "Flow"?

Before we dive into who Oshun is, let's take a moment to understand the idea of **flow**. In nature, flow is what rivers do. They twist and turn, moving over rocks and through valleys, always finding a way forward. In life, flow is when we feel connected to something greater than ourselves. It's when love comes naturally, creativity pours out of us, and we feel like we are in tune with the world.

Flow doesn't mean life is always easy. Sometimes the river hits a block or moves slowly. But it keeps going. That's the heart of Oshun's energy. She teaches us to flow with life instead of fighting against it. She helps us find sweetness even in hard times. She invites us to trust the journey, trust ourselves, and trust the unseen forces that guide us.

In this way, flow is love. It's also healing because it moves through the places that hurt and helps wash away pain. Flow is sensuality, because it allows us to enjoy our bodies and senses. And flow is power, because it gives us the strength to keep going with softness instead of force.

Who Is Oshun?

Oshun is a goddess, a spirit, and an orisha, a divine being in the Yoruba religion, which comes from West Africa. The Yoruba people have worshipped Oshun for centuries. She is one of many orishas, each of whom has their own role in the universe. Oshun's role is very special. She rules over love, rivers, beauty, fertility, joy, and harmony.

According to the old stories, Oshun is the goddess of sweet water, the rivers, streams, and fresh lakes that give life to everything around them. Just like water, Oshun brings nourishment, renewal, and peace. But she also has power. When rivers flood, they can destroy or cleanse, and Oshun can do both. She is not just gentle; she is wise, strong, and full of fire when needed.

Oshun is often shown as a beautiful woman dressed in yellow or gold, with a mirror in one hand and honey in the other. But this image is just one part of who she is. She is also a fierce protector, a healer, a dancer, a mother, and a teacher. Her stories show her as someone who helps others, but also knows how to stand up for herself.

Over time, Oshun's worship spread beyond West Africa. During the transatlantic slave trade, millions of Africans were taken to the Americas. Many carried their spiritual beliefs with them, including their devotion to Oshun. Even when they were not allowed to worship openly, they found ways to honor her. In places like Cuba, Brazil, Haiti, and the southern United States, Oshun was known by many names and was often associated with Catholic saints as a means of hiding her true identity. Despite all the hardship, her energy remained strong.

Today, Oshun is loved and honored around the world. People from all backgrounds feel her presence. Some follow traditional African religions, while others discover Oshun through art, dreams, or personal spiritual paths. She continues to speak to the human heart, across cultures and generations.

Why Oshun Matters Today

So why should we care about Oshun in today's world?

Because we live in a time when love often feels broken, when many people feel disconnected from themselves and others. We live in a world that praises control and power, but often overlooks the importance of softness, beauty, and joy. We rush through our days, forgetting to breathe. We forget to listen to our hearts.

Oshun reminds us of what we've lost, and what we can still find. She brings us back to what truly matters: connection, kindness, beauty, balance, and love.

She also reminds us of the sacred feminine, the power of being in tune with emotions, cycles, and the natural world. Whether you are a woman, a man, or a non-binary person, we all carry both feminine and masculine energy. Oshun helps us honor the part of ourselves that is gentle, intuitive, creative, and full of compassion.

Oshun also speaks to people who have been pushed aside by society, especially Black women, LGBTQ+ folks, and others who are told they must be hard to survive. She says, *"Your softness is your strength. Your joy is your birthright. You don't have to become bitter to be powerful."*

In that way, Oshun is more than a goddess. She is a way of living.

What This Book Is (and What It's Not)

This book is written with love and respect. It's not a religious rulebook or a scholarly history. It doesn't claim to speak for all traditions or all practitioners. The Yoruba religion and its diasporic forms are living systems with many branches, teachers, and paths. This book honors that diversity.

Instead, think of this as a gentle guide, an invitation to get to know Oshun in a personal and heart-centered way. It draws from stories, rituals, symbols, and spiritual insight, weaving them together into something anyone can understand. It is a book of beauty, power, and practice.

If something in these pages resonates with you, hold it close. If something doesn't feel right, it's okay to leave it behind. Your relationship with Oshun will be your own. And she welcomes all who come to her with honesty and love.

A Blessing to Begin

Before we begin, let's offer a simple blessing:

Oshun, sweet mother of the rivers,

Goddess of golden joy,

We call on your name with respect and gratitude.

Bless the reader of this book.

Fill their heart with kindness.

Guide their spirit into balance.

Teach them how to love, how to flow,

and how to live with beauty and grace.

Ashe.

Oshun invites us into a different way of being, a life guided by flow instead of force, by sweetness instead of struggle, and by joy instead of fear. That doesn't mean life becomes perfect. It means we begin to trust ourselves. We begin to see beauty again. We begin to feel alive.

As you read this book, let it be a journey into the river, a sacred, flowing river that runs through your soul. You may find healing. You may find laughter. You may even find love.

And most importantly, you may find yourself.

So, let's begin, softly, deeply, and with an open heart.

Let's walk together into the sweet waters of Oshun.

1

THE ORIGINS AND MYTHOLOGY OF OSHUN

BEFORE THE WORLD WAS FULL OF RIVERS AND SONGS, BEFORE people learned how to love and heal, there was Oshun. She was more than a spirit, she was a force. She flowed with beauty, wisdom, and strength. In the beginning, she was the sweetness the world didn't know it needed.

This chapter will guide you into Oshun's origins and stories, explaining her role in Yoruba spirituality, her powerful myths, and how her connections with other orishas show her importance in the world. Whether you're new to African traditional religion or simply curious about the origins of Oshun, this is where her sacred story begins.

Oshun in Yoruba Cosmology

Oshun originates from the Yoruba religion, one of the world's oldest and most enduring spiritual systems. The Yoruba people come from a region in West Africa that includes present-day Nigeria, Benin, and Togo. Their spiritual system is based on the belief in many divine beings known as orishas.

At the top of this spiritual system is Olodumare, the supreme creator. Olodumare is neither male nor female, but contains both. They are the source of all energy, life, and wisdom. While Olodumare created the universe, the orishas were sent to oversee and manage various aspects of it.

Oshun is one of these orishas. She was chosen by Olodumare to bring joy, balance, fertility, love, and beauty into the world. Her work is not just emotional or symbolic, it is deeply physical. Oshun makes crops grow, babies be born, and hearts find connection. She is often referred to as the orisha of sweet waters, encompassing rivers, streams, and freshwater lakes.

She is also a daughter of Olodumare, created with both tenderness and fire. Though people often see her as gentle and loving, she is not weak. She knows her worth, and the ancient stories show that she will fight for it when necessary. Oshun is proof that love is not soft because it is weak; love is soft because it is strong enough not to be hard.

The Element of Water and the Gift of Fertility

Oshun is deeply tied to water, especially rivers. In Yoruba belief, each orisha is associated with a specific element. For Oshun, water is not just something she rules, it is something she is. Water flows, heals, reflects, and nourishes. Like Oshun, water finds its way even through the hardest stone.

Water is also tied to fertility, and this is another of Oshun's gifts. Fertility does not only mean having children. It also means having ideas, dreams, growth, and joy. Oshun gives life to everything she touches. In fact, in many stories, without Oshun, the Earth would be unable to grow food or support human life.

In ceremonies, people honor her with fresh water, honey, oranges, and yellow flowers. These gifts represent her sweet and giving nature. But her power goes beyond symbols. People pray to Oshun for help with pregnancy, health, love, and emotional healing. Her water cleanses the body and spirit. Her name is whispered when new life is needed.

Oshun Creates the Rivers and Saves the World

One of the most famous stories about Oshun begins with a world in crisis.

In the time of beginnings, Olodumare sent 17 orishas to create the Earth. These included powerful figures such as Ogun (the orisha of iron and war), Obatala (the orisha of wisdom and creation), and Shango (the orisha of thunder and fire). Oshun was the only female orisha among them.

At first, the male orishas ignored her. They believed they could build the world without her help. They thought strength, tools, and force were enough. But as they worked, nothing grew. The rivers were dry. The land was barren. The sky held no rain. Animals refused to appear, and people could not survive.

The male orishas returned to Olodumare confused and ashamed. They admitted that their efforts had failed. Olodumare told them that they had made a grave mistake; they had left out Oshun, the orisha of sweetness, life, and flow.

When Oshun stepped forward, she took her mirror and honey. She danced. She sang. She poured her energy into the world. And suddenly, the Earth responded. Rivers flowed. Trees grew. Flowers bloomed. Birds sang. Humanity had a chance.

This myth teaches a deep lesson: without feminine energy, the world cannot survive. Power is not only strength; it is love, grace, creativity, and flow. Oshun did not force life into the Earth. She invited it. And life accepted her invitation.

Oshun and Her Divine Relationships

Oshun's myths are not just about her powers. They are also about her relationships with other orishas. These stories reveal her complex and powerful nature. She is not just sweet; she is strong, clever, and deeply connected to others.

Let's look at three important orishas in her life: Shango, Ogun, and Obatala.

Oshun and Shango: Fire Meets Water

Shango is the orisha of lightning, thunder, dance, and passion. He is known for his strength, charm, and intensity. In many stories, Shango and Oshun are lovers.

Their relationship is full of energy. Shango brings fire. Oshun brings water. Together, they create steam, which symbolizes transformation and power. Where Shango is bold and loud, Oshun is graceful and wise. She helps calm his storms, and he honors her beauty and intelligence.

Their love is not perfect; it faces challenges, like many great relationships. But it shows the importance of balance. We all carry both fire and water within us. We all need passion and peace. Shango and Oshun teach that powerful love is about honoring differences and working together in harmony.

Oshun and Ogun: Peace Over War

Ogun is the orisha of iron, metalwork, tools, and war. He is a builder and a fighter. He clears paths and breaks through obstacles. However, he sometimes struggles to control his anger and power.

In one myth, Ogun became so frustrated with the other orishas that he ran into the forest and refused to come back. Without him, tools could not be made. Work stopped. The world became stuck.

None of the orishas could bring him back, until Oshun came. She took her honey and mirror and went into the forest. She spoke gently, sang to him, and reminded him of his purpose. Her voice was soft, but her words were strong.

Moved by her kindness and courage, Ogun returned to his duties. Oshun did not fight him. She reached his heart. This story reminds us that peace can be more powerful than force. Oshun's wisdom shows that healing doesn't always come through battle, sometimes it comes through love.

Oshun and Obatala: Wisdom and Grace

Obatala is the orisha of wisdom, peace, and clarity. He is known for creating human bodies out of clay, which Olodumare fills with life. Obatala is calm, fair, and thoughtful. His relationship with Oshun is one of mutual respect and admiration.

Oshun and Obatala often work together in the myths. When the world is in chaos, Obatala brings logic, and Oshun brings emotion. Together, they help bring back order and harmony. Some stories even say that Oshun helped Obatala understand the importance of emotions in making wise decisions.

Their connection shows that true leadership comes from both the head and the heart. Obatala's wisdom and Oshun's grace are two sides of the same coin. Both are needed for a just and beautiful world.

The Many Forms of Oshun

In Yoruba belief, orishas have multiple forms or "paths," which reflect different aspects of their personalities. Oshun is no exception. She appears in many ways, depending on the lesson, the devotee, or the situation.

For example:

- **Oshun Ibu Kole** is the fierce protector of women and the poor.
- **Oshun Ibu Ikole** is a messenger who uses birds to carry messages to heaven.
- **Oshun Ibu Aña** is closely associated with music and the sacred drum.

These forms demonstrate the multidimensional nature of Oshun. She is not just one thing. She is softness and strength, joy and fire, beauty and protection. She changes like a river, constantly flowing, always alive.

Why Oshun's Myths Still Matter

Why are these old stories still told today? The answer is simple: they still speak to the human heart.

Oshun teaches that emotions are not weaknesses. Love is not silly. Sensuality is not shameful. Fertility is not just physical, it is the ability to create and nourish all kinds of life.

She shows us how to balance strength with softness, how to stand firm while staying kind. Her myths remind us that the world needs beauty just as much as it needs power. Without sweetness, even the strongest world becomes dry and lifeless.

Oshun's stories help us see the divine in ourselves, especially in the parts we are taught to hide. She says, *"You are sacred. Your joy matters. Your heart is a river. Let it flow."*

In the Yoruba pantheon, Oshun is not a side character. She is essential. She brings life, heals wounds, balances fire, and leads with her heart.

From creating rivers to calming angry orishas, from guiding women to helping humanity survive, Oshun's power is everywhere. She flows in our relationships, our dreams, and our hopes. When we honor Oshun, we honor the parts of ourselves that are joyful, creative, loving, and alive.

In the chapters that follow, we'll go deeper into her symbols, her worship, and how to walk with her in daily life. But as you continue reading, remember this: Oshun didn't just help create the world; she helps it bloom every single day.

Ashe.

OSHUN'S SYMBOLS, COLORS, AND SACRED NUMBERS

Symbols have the power to tell stories without using words. They hold meaning, emotion, and energy. In the spiritual world of the Yoruba religion, symbols are more than decorations; they are bridges between the divine and human worlds. For Oshun, one of the most beloved orishas, her symbols carry deep lessons about beauty, power, love, and the flow of life.

Through these sacred signs, you'll come to understand Oshun in a more personal and powerful way.

The Power of Symbols

Every orisha has symbols that connect them to the physical world. These objects are not random. They carry the energy of the orisha and help their followers feel closer to them. For Oshun, her symbols reflect her role as the goddess of love, sweetness, beauty, fertility, and rivers.

Let's look at the symbols that appear most often when honoring Oshun.

Mirrors: Reflection and Self-Love

Oshun is often shown holding a mirror in her hand. The mirror is not a symbol of vanity; it is a tool of reflection. Oshun encourages people to know themselves, not just on the outside, but also within.

When you look into a mirror, you see more than your face. You can see your emotions, your thoughts, and your truth. Oshun's mirror invites people to love who they are and to accept their natural beauty. It also teaches honesty. By reflecting the truth, the mirror helps people grow and develop.

Devotees often place mirrors on Oshun's altars or carry small ones as a reminder to practice self-love, confidence, and awareness. Looking into a mirror while praying to Oshun can help deepen the spiritual connection and create a moment of personal healing and transformation.

Honey: Sweetness, Attraction, and Healing

Honey is one of the most important offerings given to Oshun. It represents her sweet nature and her ability to heal with kindness and love. In Yoruba stories, Oshun uses honey to solve problems and calm anger. Its golden color matches her energy, and its taste reminds us that life should have sweetness.

Honey is also a symbol of attraction. Just as bees are drawn to flowers, love and abundance are drawn to sweetness. Devotees use honey in rituals when asking Oshun to help them with love, peace, or healing.

Honey can be placed on an altar, added to bath water during cleansing rituals, or used to anoint objects with intention. Some even taste a small amount of honey during prayer to invite Oshun's blessings into their body and spirit.

Gold: Abundance, Light, and Royalty

Gold is more than a color to Oshun; it is part of her essence. It shines, it glows, and it draws attention. In the Yoruba tradition, gold stands for wealth, prosperity, warmth, and divine light. Oshun is often depicted wearing golden robes, adorned with jewelry, or surrounded by gold-colored objects.

Gold also connects Oshun to her role as a queen among the orishas. She is not just beautiful, she is powerful and respected. Her gold reminds us that we are all worthy of abundance, dignity, and success.

People honor Oshun by offering gold jewelry, coins, or items painted with gold. Even if it's not made of real gold, the symbolism is what matters. Gold candles, fabrics, or beads are often used during rituals and celebrations to call in her energy of richness and joy.

Peacocks: Beauty and Watchfulness

Peacocks are one of Oshun's sacred animals. These birds are renowned for their vibrant feathers and graceful walk. Like Oshun, they carry themselves with elegance and pride.

The peacock is a symbol of beauty, vision, and alertness. Its bright eyes on its feathers represent awareness and protection. Oshun, as a guardian of love and femininity, watches over her followers the same way the peacock keeps an eye on its surroundings.

Images or statues of peacocks are placed on altars or worn as jewelry by devotees. The bird reminds people to honor their inner beauty, to stand tall, and to trust their instincts. Just like the peacock doesn't hide its feathers, Oshun encourages people to shine without shame.

Fans: Movement and Grace

Fans are another item closely linked with Oshun. In traditional Yoruba dance and ritual, fans are used to represent wind, flow, and elegance. When devotees wave a fan during a ceremony, it's as if they are calling Oshun into the space.

The fan represents the graceful movement of air, which complements Oshun's connection to flowing water. It is also a symbol of comfort and care. In hot weather, fans cool the body. In spiritual practice, they cool the spirit. Oshun uses the fan to bring calm where there is heat and to stir energy where it is stuck.

Fans can be decorated with gold, feathers, or beads. They are used in dance, prayer, and ritual to help move energy and express respect to Oshun.

River Water: Life, Cleansing, and Flow

Oshun is the orisha of rivers. Flowing, sweet water is her sacred element. It brings life to the Earth, cleanses the body, and connects the spirit to the divine. Rivers are not just places of worship; they are part of Oshun herself.

In many Yoruba and Afro-Diasporic traditions, people visit rivers to communicate with Oshun, offer gifts, and receive her blessings. Water is collected in bottles for use at home, such as for bathing, cleansing rituals, or sprinkling around a sacred space.

River water symbolizes movement, healing, and spiritual renewal. When someone is feeling lost, stuck, or overwhelmed, Oshun's waters are believed to help wash away pain and open a new path. In this way, her rivers are both physical and spiritual tools of transformation.

The Colors of Oshun

Just like her symbols, Oshun's colors carry important meanings.

Her primary colors are yellow, gold, amber, and coral. Each one reflects a different part of her personality and spiritual power.

Yellow: Joy and Vitality

Yellow is Oshun's most popular and recognizable color. It stands for joy, warmth, energy, and happiness. Like the sun, yellow brings light to dark places. It reminds us of new beginnings, growth, and the playful side of life.

Devotees wear yellow clothes, light yellow candles, or decorate their homes in yellow to invite Oshun's joyful energy. It's a color that lifts the spirit and opens the heart.

Gold: Divine Light and Abundance

Gold represents Oshun's regal nature and her connection to wealth and prosperity. It also reflects her ability to illuminate the path ahead, bringing clarity, confidence, and direction.

Gold is used in ceremonies, offerings, and spiritual jewelry to draw in Oshun's blessings of success, prosperity, and honor. It is the color of celebration, transformation, and power.

Amber: Strength and Warmth

Amber, a deep golden-orange, reflects Oshun's earthy, passionate side. It combines the brightness of gold with the grounded energy of the Earth. Amber stands for strength, warmth, and healing.

Wearing amber beads or placing amber stones on an altar can help bring calm and strength during difficult times. It's especially used in rituals for emotional support, fertility, and spiritual protection.

Coral: Feminine Power and Protection

Coral, a rich reddish-orange color, connects Oshun to the depths of the sea and to feminine wisdom. It is a color of life force, passion, and protection. Coral is often used in necklaces or bracelets worn by priestesses and devotees.

This color reminds us that Oshun is not only soft and gentle; she is also a fierce protector. She fights for justice, guards the innocent, and defends the beauty of life. Coral carries the energy of a bold, loving mother.

The Sacred Number 5

Oshun's most important number is five (5). In Yoruba spirituality, numbers are believed to hold energy and carry significant meaning. The number five represents balance, harmony, creation, and wholeness.

Why five? Think about your own body. You have five fingers on each hand, five toes on each foot, and five main senses. This number shows up in the natural world to remind us of the perfect balance between the physical and the spiritual.

In rituals, offerings to Oshun are often arranged in groups of five:

- Five oranges
- Five candles
- Five coins
- Five flowers

This pattern helps align the ritual with Oshun's energy. The number five also reminds devotees that love, healing, and abundance come when everything is in balance, mind, body, spirit, heart, and soul.

How Devotees Use These Symbols in Daily Life

You don't need to be part of a temple or have a priestess to connect with Oshun. Her energy is everywhere, and her symbols can be used in simple ways to bring her closer.

Creating Sacred Space

Many people create a small altar or sacred space to honor Oshun. This might include:

- A bowl of river water
- A yellow or gold candle
- A mirror
- A few drops of honey
- Yellow or amber flowers
- A piece of gold or coral jewelry

These items don't have to be expensive. What matters most is the intention behind them. Devotees may say a prayer, write a note of gratitude, or simply sit in silence, inviting Oshun's presence into their day.

Wearing Her Colors

Some devotees wear yellow, gold, or coral when they want to feel Oshun's energy. Wearing these colors can help bring confidence, attraction, and joy into their life. It's also a quiet way to honor Oshun throughout the day, especially when going into difficult situations or needing emotional strength.

Offering with Love

Giving offerings is a way to build a relationship with Oshun. People might leave honey on a plate, float flowers in a river, or offer a piece of jewelry to her altar. These acts are more than gifts; they are acts of love, gratitude, and respect.

The key is to offer with a full heart. Whether it's five coins or a single candle, sincerity is what Oshun responds to most.

Using Numbers in Prayer

When praying to Oshun, repeating a phrase five times or offering five thanks helps align with her energy. It brings rhythm and intention to the prayer. Some also tap their fingers five times on a sacred item or draw five circles in the air before beginning a ritual.

Symbols are powerful messengers. They help us connect with forces greater than ourselves and remind us of the beauty that lies within us. Oshun's mirrors, honey, gold, and rivers teach us to move with grace, speak with kindness, and live in harmony.

Her colors shine with meaning, lighting the way to joy, love, and self-worth. Her sacred number teaches that everything we need is already within us; we just have to find the balance.

Through these symbols, Oshun whispers, *"You are worthy of sweetness. You are made of light. Flow like the river, and you will always find your way."*

Ashe.

3

ROADS OF OSHUN

In Yoruba and Afro-Diasporic traditions, the orishas are not one-dimensional. Each one carries many different faces, moods, and powers. These different forms are referred to as roads, also known as Caminos in Spanish or avatars in certain spiritual practices.

Think of it like this, Oshun is one divine being, but she shows herself in many ways. Just like water can become rain, mist, or a rushing river, Oshun appears in different forms depending on what is needed. Some roads of Oshun are gentle and sweet, others are fiery and bold. Some bring healing, while others demand justice.

In this chapter, we will explore the roads of Oshun, focusing on who they are, what they do, and how people connect with them. These unique aspects help us see the full picture of Oshun, not just as a goddess of love and beauty, but as a powerful and complex spirit who holds many truths.

What Are "Roads" of Oshun?

In Yoruba belief and its branches, such as Santería and Candomblé, a "road" refers to a specific manifestation of an orisha. Each road has its own personality, strengths, weaknesses, colors, offerings, and lessons. These different forms help Oshun connect with the diverse needs of her followers.

For example:

- Someone who needs healing from heartbreak may connect with the nurturing road of Oshun.
- Someone seeking justice might call on the road of Oshun, known for power and anger.
- A devotee who wants to deepen their spiritual connection might work with a wise and mystical form of Oshun.

The roads are not separate goddesses; they are faces of the same divine being. They allow Oshun to serve the world in different ways, depending on what each person or situation calls for.

Ibu Kole: The Collector of Dust

One of the most important and well-known roads of Oshun is Ibu Kole.

Meaning and Role

The name "Kole" means "to gather or collect." Ibu Kole is often described as the Oshun who collects dust from the Earth, which may seem like a simple act, but it's deeply symbolic. In mythology, she used this dust to create paths, solve problems, and fight injustice.

Ibu Kole is a warrior, a defender, and a wise strategist. Though she still carries Oshun's sweetness, she is also deep, grounded, and serious.

Appearance

Ibu Kole is often dressed in dark golds or earthy yellows, featuring symbols such as feathers, dust, or dry leaves. She is associated with the vulture, a sacred bird that represents wisdom, patience, and survival.

Energy and Use

Devotees call on Ibu Kole when they need protection, guidance in difficult times, or support during conflict. She is especially helpful when someone is being mistreated or ignored, because she reminds people of their worth and teaches them to rise above their struggles.

Ibu Ikole: The Messenger of Transformation

Ibu Ikole is another powerful road. Her name is often translated as "She who sends messages" or "Messenger of the Earth."

Meaning and Role

Ibu Ikole is renowned for serving as a bridge between the spirit world and the earthly realm. She sends messages between the orishas and humans. In some traditions, she is closely linked to the vulture, just like Ibu Kole. Still, her main role is communication and transformation.

She is also believed to have played a significant role in bringing civilization to the world, teaching people how to live in harmony and with respect.

Appearance

Ibu Ikole may wear feathers, especially those of a vulture, and is often surrounded by objects related to communication, such as bells, fans, or birds.

Energy and Use

People turn to Ibu Ikole when they are seeking answers, direction, or clarity. She is called during times of confusion, important decisions, or spiritual growth. She helps people receive messages from their ancestors or the divine.

Ibu Aña: The Oshun of the Drums

Ibu Aña is the road of Oshun that dances to the beat of the drum.

Meaning and Role

The word "Aña" refers to the sacred drum, and Ibu Aña is deeply connected to music, rhythm, and ceremony. She is a lively and joyful manifestation of Oshun. Where she goes, celebration and beauty follow.

This road teaches that music is not just entertainment; it is a powerful spiritual tool. The sound of the drum awakens the spirit and connects people to the divine.

Appearance

Ibu Aña is usually seen wearing bright yellow, gold, and even red, symbolizing her passion and creative fire. She may be holding or dancing near the drums.

Energy and Use

Devotees call on Ibu Aña when they want to celebrate life, express creative energy, or connect with the joy of being alive. She is also helpful during healing rituals, where rhythm and dance are used to release emotional pain from the body.

Ibu Yumu: The Gentle and Silent Healer

Ibu Yumu is one of Oshun's most peaceful and nurturing roads.

Meaning and Role

Ibu Yumu is soft, quiet, and motherly. She does not raise her voice or bring storms. Instead, she heals through silence, love, and comfort. Her presence is like the calm after a storm, the warm hug that makes everything feel better.

She is often connected to childbirth, midwifery, and caring for the vulnerable.

Appearance

Ibu Yumu may wear light yellow, cream, or white. Her symbols include linen, lace, soft fabrics, and natural items like river stones or flowers.

Energy and Use

People seek out Ibu Yumu when they need emotional healing, especially after trauma, grief, or loss. She brings patience, rest, and renewal.

Ibu D'Omi: The Oshun of Deep Waters

This is the Oshun who lives in the depths of the river, where the water is cold, still, and full of mystery.

Meaning and Role

Ibu D'Omi is a deeply spiritual and powerful version of Oshun. She holds secrets and teaches about the unseen world. She is not as bright and open as some of the other roads, but her depth and wisdom are unmatched.

Appearance

She is associated with dark gold, navy blue, and occasionally black. Her energy is calm but intense. Her symbols may include shells, stones, and deep river water.

Energy and Use

Devotees visit Ibu D'Omi for spiritual guidance, meditation, and shadow work. She helps people understand their inner world and teaches that true power often comes from the places we fear or hide.

Ibu Ololodi: The Wise and Protective Partner

Oshun has many romantic relationships in mythology, and on the road of Ibu Ololodi, she appears as the wife of Orunmila, the orisha of wisdom and divination.

Meaning and Role

Ibu Ololodi is intelligent, practical, and protective. She knows how to read signs, understand people, and offer advice. As the partner of the wise orisha, she is not ruled by emotion but by insight and clarity.

Appearance

She is often depicted wearing yellow and green, colors associated with growth and balance. She may carry items used in divination, like cowrie shells or a sacred mat.

Energy and Use

People turn to Ibu Ololodi when they need mental strength, help making choices, or protection from spiritual confusion. She is like a wise aunt or godmother who helps you see clearly.

Other Roads of Oshun (Briefly Introduced)

There are many more roads of Oshun, each with its own mysteries. Here are a few others worth mentioning:

- **Ibu Arogba** – A road linked to ritual purification and sacred baths.
- **Ibu Oku** – A darker road, sometimes connected to death, loss, or mourning. She teaches how to rise again after sorrow.
- **Ibu Sekese** – A playful and flirtatious road, full of charm and sensual power.
- **Ibu Agandara** – A strong road that fights for justice, especially for women and children.
- **Ibu Miya** – A watery road connected to dreams and prophecy, often working through symbols in sleep or visions.

Comparing the Roads of Oshun

Below is a chart to help you compare some of Oshun's roads:

Road Name Main Traits Colors Specialties Symbols

Ibu Kole Warrior, grounded, just Earthy golds, yellow Protection, overcoming struggle, Vulture, dust

Ibu Ikole Messenger, wise, guiding, Yellow, gray, Spiritual messages, direction, Feathers, birds

Ibu Aña Joyful, musical, expressive, Yellow, red, gold Dance, healing through rhythm Drums, bells

Ibu Yumu Gentle, healing, comforting Cream, soft yellow Emotional care, motherhood Lace, water, stones

Ibu D'Omi Deep, introspective, mystical Navy, black, gold Meditation, shadow work River shells, stones

Ibu Ololodi Wise, balanced, protective, Yellow, green Divination, mental clarity Cowrie shells, sacred mat

Ibu Oku Intense, transformative, mournful Dark yellow, purple Death, rebirth, grieving River mud, black stones

Ibu Sekese Flirtatious, attractive, fun-loving Bright gold, coral Love, seduction, feminine power Perfume, sweets

Ibu Agandara Bold, strong, justice-driven Red, gold Fighting injustice, empowering women Fan, shield

Ibu Miya Mysterious, dreamy, prophetic Aqua, soft blue Dreams, vision, night work Moon charms, water bowls

How Practitioners Work With Oshun's Roads

Working with a specific road of Oshun is like building a relationship with a very specific part of her spirit. In many traditions, especially Lucumí/Santería or Candomblé, only trained priests or initiated devotees are allowed to identify a person's road of Oshun through divination. However, non-initiated individuals can still respectfully honor Oshun by learning about her various paths and calling on the ones that align with their needs.

Here are some gentle ways to work with Oshun's roads:

- **Pray using her name**: *"Oshun Ibu Kole, give me strength and courage today."*
- **Decorate your altar** with colors and symbols tied to that road.

- **Study her stories**: Learn her lessons and apply them to your life.
- **Make offerings** that match the energy of the road you are calling on.

Most of all, approach each road with respect and curiosity. Oshun is always listening, and each path she walks has something special to teach you.

The roads of Oshun are like pages in a sacred book, each one reveals a different part of her wisdom, power, and love. Some are joyful, some are fierce, and some are full of mystery. Together, they show us that Oshun is not just a goddess of beauty; she is a whole universe of emotion, strength, and transformation.

By learning her roads, you learn to understand yourself. Whether you're seeking peace, passion, truth, or guidance, Oshun has a path for you to walk.

In the next chapter, we'll explore how Oshun is honored in traditional Yoruba religion, and how her roads come to life in temples, rituals, and communities worldwide.

4

OSHUN IN YORUBA SPIRITUAL LIFE

IN THE HEART OF WEST AFRICA, IN THE LAND WE KNOW TODAY as Nigeria, the Yoruba people have worshipped Oshun for centuries. Long before she became known around the world through art, music, or popular culture, Oshun was, and still is, a living presence in Yoruba religious life. She is more than just a symbol of love and beauty. She is a powerful orisha, a sacred river goddess, and a key figure in the Ifá system, one of the world's oldest spiritual traditions.

This chapter will take you into the heart of Yoruba land to explore how Oshun is honored in traditional ways. You'll learn how she fits into the spiritual structure of the Yoruba religion, the role of priests and priestesses, the ceremonies and festivals held in her name, and why the Osun-Osogbo Sacred Grove is one of the most important spiritual places on Earth.

Who Are the Orishas in Yoruba Belief?

To understand Oshun's role in Yoruba spiritual life, we must first understand the orishas.

In Yoruba religion, there is one supreme creator, Olódùmarè. Olódùmarè is the source of all life, light, and wisdom. But instead of interacting directly with every part of the world, Olódùmarè works through orishas, divine spirits that help guide, protect, and care for humanity.

There are hundreds of orishas. Some are warriors. Some are healers. Others rule over elements like wind, fire, or water. Each orisha has its own personality, powers, colors, foods, and rituals. They are like divine family members, each with their own role to play in the spiritual universe.

Oshun is one of the most loved orishas. She rules over the river, but her energy also touches beauty, fertility, healing, and love. She brings sweetness into the world, like honey flowing into water.

The Ifá System and Oshun's Sacred Role

The spiritual tradition of the Yoruba people is called Ifá. It is a system of divination, worship, and wisdom that has been passed down for thousands of years. At the heart of Ifá is Orunmila, the orisha of wisdom, who helps people understand the messages of fate.

In Ifá, every person is believed to be born under the guidance of a particular orisha. This orisha becomes their guardian spirit, walking with them throughout life. For many people, that guardian is Oshun.

Oshun plays a major role in the Ifá system. While she is not a diviner like Orunmila, she is often consulted during divination sessions due to her ability to understand the emotional aspects of a person's life. She brings balance where there is conflict and helps solve problems that require love, kindness, or beauty to fix.

When people seek help from the Ifá oracle, they may be told to make offerings to Oshun or visit her river. This demonstrates her profound impact on guiding people's lives, even when she doesn't speak through the oracle directly. She brings blessings to those who follow the right path.

Priests and Priestesses: Babalawos and Iyalorishas

Yoruba spirituality is not practiced alone. It is passed down and protected by exceptional spiritual leaders. These leaders include:

Babalawos

A Babalawo is a high priest of Ifá, trained in the ancient art of divination. These wise men study for many years, learning verses from the Odu Ifá, a sacred text comprising over 250 spiritual stories or signs.

Babalawos use tools like palm nuts or a chain called the Opelè to speak with the spirit world. If someone is experiencing trouble in life, such as illness, confusion, or family problems, they may seek guidance from a Babalawo.

Though Oshun is not a leading voice in the Odu Ifá, Babalawos will often recommend offerings or rituals to honor her if her presence is needed to heal or solve a situation.

Iyalorishas

An Iyalorisha is a priestess devoted to a particular orisha, and "Iya" means "mother" in Yoruba. An Iyalorisha dedicated to Oshun is referred to as an Oshun priestess, and she dedicates her life to serving the river goddess.

Iyalorishas are known for:

- Leading rituals

- Teaching younger devotees
- Healing through herbs, water, and song
- Interpreting dreams and spiritual signs

A child who is chosen by Oshun may be trained by an Iyalorisha, learning how to serve the goddess through prayer, dance, and ritual.

The Community Role

Both Babalawos and Iyalorishas play crucial roles in the spiritual well-being of their communities. They make sure that the connection between people and orishas remains strong. When people are out of balance, emotionally, spiritually, or physically, these leaders help restore harmony, often by working with Oshun's sweet and loving energy.

Shrines, Altars, and Sacred Places

In Yoruba land, Oshun is not just worshipped in temples. She is honored in nature, especially near rivers, streams, and springs. One of the most powerful ways to connect with Oshun is to visit her river, speak to her out loud, and leave an offering by the water.

Many communities build shrines to Oshun, which may be located in homes, village centers, or near rivers. These shrines often include:

- A bowl of clean water
- Honey, oranges, or other sweet offerings
- A small mirror or fan
- Symbols of fertility and beauty

At the shrine, people pray, sing, and ask Oshun for blessings. Women who are trying to have children may leave special gifts. Children may dance and clap near the water, celebrating her with joy and laughter.

In homes, people also create personal altars to Oshun. These are decorated in her favorite colors, yellow, gold, and amber, and kept clean to show respect. Devotees may light candles, place flowers, or leave a cup of honey every day as an offering.

Ceremonies and Rituals in Oshun's Honor

Ceremonies for Oshun are often rich in music, dance, food, and sacred rituals. They can be small or large, personal or public, but they are always done with care and love.

Naming Ceremonies

When a child is born, it is common to ask the orishas to bless the new life. If Oshun is the guardian orisha of the child, special prayers and gifts are offered to her at a nearby river. The child may be given a name that honors Oshun, such as "Osunbunmi" (meaning "Oshun gave me this") or "Osuntola" (meaning "Oshun is wealth").

Healing Ceremonies

If someone is sick, sad, or going through a hard time, a priest or priestess may lead a healing ceremony in Oshun's name. This could include:

- A ritual bath with herbs and river water
- A prayer asking Oshun to remove sorrow
- Dancing and singing her songs to lift the spirit

Oshun is known for softening the heart, helping people let go of pain and find their way back to joy.

Festivals

The largest and most renowned celebration of Oshun is the Osun-Osogbo Festival. This annual event attracts thousands of people from around the world.

The Osun-Osogbo Sacred Grove

On the edge of the city of Osogbo, along the Osun River, lies a sacred forest known as the Osun-Osogbo Sacred Grove. This is one of the last remaining sacred groves in Yoruba land, and it is the most important site for worshipping Oshun.

The Grove is filled with:

- Ancient trees and wildlife
- Statues and shrines dedicated to Oshun and other orishas
- Sacred paths where rituals and offerings take place

This place is more than a forest; it is believed to be Oshun's spiritual home. It is where she first made a pact with the people of Osogbo, promising to protect them if they would honor her and care for the river.

In 2005, the Osun-Osogbo Grove was designated a UNESCO World Heritage Site due to its profound cultural and spiritual significance. It is protected and cared for by priestesses, artists, and spiritual guardians who keep Oshun's traditions alive.

The Osun-Osogbo Festival

Every year, in August, the Osun-Osogbo Festival is held to honor the goddess. For two whole weeks, the city of Osogbo is alive with dancing, drumming, and prayer.

Opening Ceremonies

The festival begins with a purification ceremony called Iwopopo, which clears away any bad energy from the town. Next comes the Ina Olujumerindinlogun, the lighting of a sacred 16-point lamp that represents peace and spiritual light.

Rituals at the River

One of the most powerful moments is when the Arugba, a chosen virgin girl, carries offerings to the river on her head. She is led through the town in a grand parade, followed by priests, kings, and thousands of worshippers.

People gather along the riverbanks, singing songs like:

"Osun mi, Osun mi, gbe mi lo!"

("My Oshun, my Oshun, carry me away!")

Offerings of honey, fruits, and flowers are placed in the river as prayers are spoken aloud.

Community Celebration

Throughout the festival, people wear yellow and white, dance to talking drums, cook feasts, and share stories of Oshun's past miracles. It is a time of unity, joy, and reflection, a moment when all come together to express gratitude to Oshun for her blessings.

Why Oshun Matters in Everyday Life

For Yoruba people, Oshun is not just honored during festivals or rituals. She is present in everyday life.

- A mother may pray to Oshun before giving birth.
- A farmer may thank Oshun after a good harvest.
- A young person may leave a gift at the river when searching for love.
- An elder may pour water on the ground to call her name during a blessing.

Oshun is with her people in the river's song, the warmth of the sun, the laughter of children, and the sweetness of honey. She reminds people to live with grace, kindness, and balance, even in the most challenging times.

Respecting the Traditions

As Oshun's name becomes more popular around the world, it is important to remember that her worship is part of a sacred tradition. These practices have been protected for generations by Yoruba elders, priests, and communities.

Learning about Oshun should always be done with humility and respect. If you are not part of the tradition but want to honor her, take time to study, listen, and show gratitude for what you receive.

Oshun's Place in Yoruba Spiritual Life

Oshun is a powerful orisha in the Yoruba religion. She is honored in the Ifá system, where her guidance helps people live better lives. Her followers include both priests and everyday people, who come to her for healing, wisdom, and joy.

Her presence can be felt:

- In river ceremonies and household shrines
- Through festivals like the Osun-Osogbo celebration
- In the quiet prayers of mothers, lovers, and seekers of peace

The Osun-Osogbo Sacred Grove is her spiritual home, a place where the natural world and the divine meet. There, her energy flows freely, just like the river that carries her name.

DIASPORA DEVOTION FROM SANTERÍA, CANDOMBLÉ, AND BEYOND

WHEN PEOPLE SPEAK OF OSHUN TODAY, THEY OFTEN ENVISION her in various forms. In Nigeria, she is honored as the orisha of the river, beauty, and fertility. In Cuba, she is called Ochún and worshipped in Santería. In Brazil, she is known as Oxum in the Candomblé religion. In Haiti, Trinidad, the Dominican Republic, and other parts of the Caribbean and the Americas, her energy is known by many names and traditions.

How did Oshun travel so far from her homeland? Why does she appear with different names, outfits, and customs in so many places?

The answer lies in history, specifically, in the forced movement of millions of African people across the Atlantic during the transatlantic slave trade. Though many Africans were taken from their homes, their languages, and their cultures, they carried with them something that could not be stolen: their spirits, their songs, and their orishas.

Oshun's Journey: Across the Atlantic

Between the 1500s and 1800s, millions of African people were taken from their homes and forced onto ships that sailed to the Americas. This was part of the Atlantic slave trade, one of the most painful and violent events in human history.

Many of the people enslaved and brought to the Caribbean and the Americas were from West Africa, including the Yoruba regions of present-day Nigeria and Benin. These people brought with them their languages, dances, music, and religious beliefs, especially their devotion to the orishas.

Though they were torn from their land, they were not separated from their spirits. The orishas, including Oshun, accompanied them across the ocean, hidden in memory, prayer, and ritual.

But once in the Americas, enslaved Africans were often forced to convert to Christianity by European colonizers. Practicing African religions openly was forbidden. Yet, the people found a way to keep their traditions alive.

Santería and the Birth of Ochún in Cuba

One of the most powerful examples of African religion surviving in the Americas is Santería, also known as La Regla de Ocha. This spiritual practice originated in Cuba.

Santería blends the traditional Yoruba religion with elements of Catholicism, the religion brought by Spanish colonizers. The Yoruba orishas were matched with Catholic saints, allowing enslaved people to worship their own gods in secret.

In Santería, Oshun is known as Ochún (pronounced "Oh-choon"). Though the spelling is slightly different, the essence is the same. Ochún still rules over love, beauty, fertility, and rivers. She still loves honey, gold, and yellow dresses. But in Cuba, she is also associated with Our Lady of Charity (La Virgen de la Caridad del Cobre), a form of the Virgin Mary in Catholic belief.

Our Lady of Charity

Our Lady of Charity is a beloved figure in Cuban Catholicism. She is shown wearing a golden robe, often standing on water, and she brings hope and healing to the people.

To enslaved Yoruba people in Cuba, she looked like Oshun. So, when they were told to pray to the Virgin Mary, they prayed to Oshun in secret, using the saint as a mask. This process is known as syncretism, which involves blending two distinct religious traditions together.

Because of this clever and sacred adaptation, Oshun was never forgotten in Cuba. She lived on as Ochún, protected by the image of the Virgin, honored through dance, offerings, and song, just like in Yoruba land.

Ritual and Devotion in Santería

In Santería, Ochún is still worshipped through rich ceremonies and music. Devotees, called Santeros and Santeras, honor her through:

- Drumming and dancing: Special rhythms, known as "bembé" or "toques," are played on batá drums to summon Ochún into the space.
- Offerings: Honey, cinnamon, oranges, sunflowers, and yellow clothing are given to her.
- Ritual baths: Just like in Yoruba land, water is used to cleanse and connect with her energy.

- Initiations: Those who become priests or priestesses (called Olorishas) undergo rigorous training and sacred rituals to become spiritual leaders.

Ochún's personality in Santería is sweet and loving, but she can also be fierce if disrespected. She teaches people to value themselves, love others, and stand up for justice and fairness.

Candomblé and Oxum in Brazil

In Brazil, Oshun is known as Oxum (pronounced "Oh-shoom") and is worshipped in a religion called Candomblé. Like Santería, Candomblé blends Yoruba spiritual practices with Catholic traditions, especially in the northeastern state of Bahia, where many people of African descent live.

Oxum is one of the most loved orixás (the Portuguese word for orishas) in Brazil. She is the queen of sweet waters, beauty, elegance, and love. Like Oshun, she is often shown wearing golden clothes, holding a mirror, and dancing with grace and joy.

Oxum and Catholic Saints

In Candomblé, Oxum is often linked with Nossa Senhora Aparecida (Our Lady of Aparecida), the patron saint of Brazil. This Black Madonna figure is deeply loved by Brazilians, and many of Oxum's followers also pray to her in times of need.

Through this connection, Oxum has become a symbol of strength and protection for Black women, mothers, and families in Brazil.

Worship in Candomblé

Candomblé ceremonies are lively and powerful. They often include:

- Public festivals, where people dance in white and yellow to honor Oxum
- Private rituals, where followers receive messages through divination and song
- Sacred drumming, using rhythms specific to each orixá

Oxum's temples, called Terreiros, are spiritual homes where rituals are held and orixás are honored. Devotees may spend years learning the traditions, songs, and secrets of Oxum before becoming fully initiated.

Like her Yoruba form, Oxum teaches her followers to love deeply, walk with dignity, and find strength in softness.

Other Faces of Oshun in the Diaspora

Oshun's presence can also be found in other parts of the world, where African traditions were carried and reborn in new ways.

Haiti: Ezili and the Lwa

In Haiti, the religion of Vodou (or Voodoo) includes spirits called lwa, who are similar to orishas. Oshun does not appear by name in Vodou. Still, many believe her spirit lives on in Erzulie Freda, a powerful lwa of love, beauty, and sweetness.

Erzulie Freda wears pink or gold, loves perfume and flowers, and is called on for matters of the heart. Like Oshun, she brings both joy and sorrow. She reminds her followers that love is powerful, but it can also hurt when misused.

Trinidad and the Caribbean

In Trinidad and Tobago, some communities still honor Yoruba deities through the Orisha tradition or the Shango Baptist faith, which combines African, Christian, and local practices.

Oshun is often called on for healing, family blessings, and strength. Devotees may gather near rivers, sing African songs, and wear yellow to invite her energy.

In the Dominican Republic, Puerto Rico, and Colombia, Oshun is known by different names but always appears in traditions that blend African roots with Christian forms. Sometimes she appears on spiritualist altars, surrounded by candles, roses, and glass bowls filled with water.

Survival Through Story, Music, and Art

What helped Oshun survive slavery, oppression, and time? Her story, her music, and her people.

Even when African languages were banned, people passed down the orishas through:

- Songs sung in hidden circles at night
- Dances performed during Christian festivals
- Drums that carried sacred messages
- Art and embroidery, filled with spiritual symbols

Today, the traditions are no longer hidden. In many parts of the Caribbean and Latin America, Oshun's name is spoken with pride. Her image appears in paintings, songs, and even street murals. Artists celebrate her as a symbol of resilience, beauty, and freedom.

Oshun's Rebirth in the Modern World

Over the last 50 years, more people worldwide have become familiar with Oshun through books, movies, music, and social media. In the United States and Europe, her image has been reclaimed by the African diaspora as a symbol of Black womanhood, divine femininity, and spiritual power.

In New Orleans, Atlanta, New York, and other cities with large Afro-Caribbean and Afro-Latin populations, you can find Oshun altars in homes, public festivals, and practitioners teaching traditional rituals.

Many modern devotees are reconnecting with their roots by studying Yoruba traditions, learning songs in Lucumí (the liturgical language of Santería), or visiting sacred rivers to make offerings.

Whether she is called Oshun, Ochún, Oxum, or Erzulie, her message remains the same:

Love yourself. Honor beauty. Protect your joy. Let your river flow.

6

OSHUN'S SENSUAL AND SACRED FEMININE POWER

OSHUN IS OFTEN REMEMBERED FOR HER SWEETNESS, BEAUTY, AND golden glow. She dances by rivers, wears sparkling clothes, and accepts offerings of honey, flowers, and perfume. But there is much more to her than just charm and softness.

Oshun holds a special kind of power, the power of feminine energy in its fullest form. She is sensual, loving, and confident. She knows how to express herself with grace and joy, but she also demands respect and knows her worth.

Oshun's beauty is not just physical. It is spiritual. Her sensuality is not weakness, it is strength.

Let's dive into how her feminine power can guide us in our daily lives.

Sensuality as a Sacred Gift

Sensuality refers to the use of your senses, touch, sight, taste, smell, and sound, to fully appreciate and enjoy the world around you. It's about being connected to your body and your emotions.

For Oshun, sensuality is not something to be ashamed of. It is a divine expression of joy, life, and connection.

In many cultures, people have been taught to hide their feelings, cover their bodies, or feel guilty for enjoying simple pleasures. But Oshun reminds us that our bodies are sacred. Enjoying beauty, affection, and desire is a natural part of being human. She teaches that pleasure can be a spiritual experience when it comes from love and respect.

When we dance to music that makes us feel alive, wear clothes that make us feel beautiful, or take time to care for our bodies, we are living in alignment with Oshun's energy.

Sensuality does not mean being perfect. It means being present. It's about honoring the body you have right now and finding ways to love it more each day.

The Mirror: A Symbol of Self-Love

One of Oshun's most sacred symbols is the mirror. She often holds a mirror in her artwork and statues. But she does not look into the mirror with vanity; she uses it as a tool of self-reflection and self-love.

When you look in a mirror, what do you see? Do you judge yourself, or do you appreciate who you are?

Oshun teaches that your reflection is a part of your spirit. Your outer beauty is not separate from your inner light, they work together. By looking into a mirror and loving what you see, you begin to accept your full self. That acceptance creates power.

Self-love is one of the greatest forms of strength, and Oshun is a master of it. She shows us that when we accept ourselves, we become more open to love, healing, and abundance.

A simple daily practice can be this:

- Look into a mirror and smile at yourself.
- Say kind words out loud like: *"I am beautiful. I am enough. I am radiant like the sun."*
- Over time, these small acts of love can change the way you see yourself, and the way others see you, too.

The Power of Attraction and Charisma

Oshun is known for her charm. People are drawn to her not just because of her appearance, but also because of how she carries herself. She walks with confidence, speaks with grace, and expresses herself fully. This kind of attraction is called charisma, a natural energy that draws people to you.

Charisma doesn't come from trying too hard. It comes from being comfortable in your skin. Oshun teaches that when you enjoy your own company, others will be more likely to enjoy it too.

You don't need to look or act like anyone else to be magnetic. You just need to connect with your true self, love who you are, and let your light shine.

Oshun also teaches us to take pride in our appearance, not for others, but for ourselves. Wearing clothes that make you feel good, brushing your hair, or applying a scent you love can boost your energy and attract the right people and opportunities to you.

Softness is Not Weakness

Sometimes the world tells us that to be strong, we have to be hard, tough, or aggressive. But Oshun shows another way. She teaches that softness is also a form of strength.

Water is soft, yet it shapes the land. Honey is sweet, yet it nourishes life. Flowers are delicate, yet they bloom in even the hardest soil.

Being kind, gentle, or emotional doesn't make you weak. In fact, it takes courage to show your feelings and treat others with care. Oshun's softness does not make her any less powerful, it makes her even more divine.

Her teachings remind us that we don't have to give up our gentleness to be respected. We can be graceful and still stand strong. We can cry and still be brave. We can love deeply and still protect our peace.

Body Positivity and Embodied Joy

Oshun loves the body in all its forms, big or small, young or old, smooth or scarred. She does not ask anyone to look a certain way. Instead, she invites us to celebrate our bodies as vessels of life and joy.

Many people struggle with how they feel about their bodies. Society often promotes narrow ideas of beauty that leave people feeling left out or inadequate. Oshun's presence says otherwise. She whispers, *"You are already beautiful. You don't need to change to be worthy of love."*

Body acceptance means loving yourself where you are, not just where you hope to be. It means treating your body like a friend, not an enemy.

Oshun teaches us to move our bodies with freedom through dance, swimming, stretching, and walking in nature. When we move in ways that feel good, we activate our own joy.

Her favorite place is the river, a place where people can go to cleanse, play, and release their worries. Being in or near water helps us reconnect with our bodies and release tension. Try visiting a river or beach when you can. Let the water remind you that you are alive, sacred, and worthy of love.

Seduction and Sacred Desire

Oshun is also the orisha of seduction and desire. However, she does not use seduction to manipulate; she uses it as a form of connection and creation.

Desire is not something to be feared or hidden. It is a natural part of life. It's the energy that draws people together, helps new life begin, and brings passion into everyday experiences.

Oshun teaches us that when desire comes from love and respect, it is holy. She invites us to feel pleasure without shame, to enjoy intimacy with honesty, and to set clear boundaries when needed.

In her stories, Oshun frequently employs her charm and passion to resolve problems and promote peace. She knows how to speak sweetly, how to listen deeply, and how to hold her own power.

Her lesson is this: Your desires are sacred. You can be both seductive and spiritual. You can enjoy love and still be wise. You can say yes when you want to, and no when you don't.

Beauty Rituals to Honor Oshun

One way to connect with Oshun's energy is through beauty rituals. These are simple actions that help you feel more connected to yourself and more open to love and joy.

Here are some rituals inspired by Oshun that you can try at home:

1. Honey Face Mask

Honey is one of Oshun's sacred gifts. It's natural, sweet, and healing.

What you need:

- A spoonful of raw honey
- A clean towel and warm water

What to do:

- Gently spread the honey over your face.
- As it sits, close your eyes and think of something you love about yourself.
- Rinse after 10 minutes and say: *"I honor the sweetness within me."*

2. Mirror Affirmation

Select a mirror in your room and make it a sacred space.

What to do:

- Every morning or evening, look into the mirror and say an affirmation like:
  - *"I am beautiful in body and soul."*
  - *"I shine with Oshun's light."*
  - *"I love and accept myself completely."*

Repeat daily for 7 days and notice how your energy changes.

3. Oshun Bath Ritual

What you need:

- Warm water

- A few drops of honey
- Yellow or orange flowers (like marigold or sunflower petals)
- A few drops of perfume or sweet essential oil (like rose or orange)

What to do:

- Fill a tub or large bowl with warm water.
- Add the ingredients and stir clockwise.
- Sit or stand in the water and imagine yourself surrounded by golden light.
- Whisper a prayer of self-love or a wish for confidence.

Let the water soak into your skin and carry away stress or self-doubt.

Attracting Confidence and Love

Oshun teaches that attraction begins within. If you want more love in your life, you must start by loving yourself first.

People who honor Oshun often say that once they started walking with her energy, they felt more seen, more joyful, and more in control of their lives.

Here are a few things you can do to attract love and confidence in Oshun's name:

- Wear yellow or gold to invite joy and warmth.
- Dance when you feel stressed to shift your mood.
- Give yourself compliments and accept praise from others.
- Keep a small mirror or golden charm as a reminder of your beauty.

- Speak kindly to yourself, especially during hard days.

Remember, confidence is not about being perfect. It's about trusting your voice, honoring your body, and walking with purpose, no matter how uncertain life may feel.

Oshun as a Role Model for All

Oshun's feminine power is not limited to one gender, age, or background. Anyone, no matter who they are, can learn from her. Her energy is about balance, beauty, emotional honesty, and the courage to feel.

She teaches us to:

- Celebrate our sensuality instead of hiding it.
- Love our reflection instead of criticizing it.
- Connect through kindness, not control.
- Find joy in small pleasures and share them with others.

Whether you are young or old, shy or bold, Oshun's message remains the same:

You are worthy. You are beautiful. And you are sacred.

Oshun's power lives in the way we treat ourselves. It is in the softness of our voices, the curve of a smile, the bold color of a dress, the joy in our dance, and the warmth we bring into a room.

To live in her energy is to choose beauty, not just in appearance, but in actions. It is to walk with confidence, to honor your body, to speak your truth, and to make space for love in your life.

7

STRENGTH, GRACE, AND JUSTICE OF OSHUN

OSHUN IS OFTEN CELEBRATED FOR HER BEAUTY, JOY, AND sweetness. But beneath her golden smile lies a strong and wise spirit. She is not only the goddess of love and rivers, she is also a fighter for justice, a voice for the voiceless, and a protector of what is right.

When people think of wisdom, they often imagine someone old and serious. But Oshun shows us that wisdom can be soft and fiery at the same time. She teaches through stories, actions, and energy. Her strength is not just physical, it is emotional and spiritual. It lives in her ability to feel deeply, love fully, and stand up for herself and others with confidence.

Oshun as a Warrior for Justice

Oshun may be known for her sweetness, but she is not to be taken lightly. When injustice or unfair treatment occurs, Oshun does not remain silent. She speaks up. She takes action. And she utilizes her intelligence to restore balance to the world.

One powerful story recounts how the world was once ruled by male orishas who disregarded and disrespected Oshun and the other female orishas. They believed they could manage the Earth without women's help. The world quickly fell into chaos. The crops would not grow, the rivers stopped flowing, and everything became dry and lifeless.

Oshun, watching the destruction, decided to act. Instead of fighting with anger, she used her cleverness. She went to Olodumare, the supreme creator, and explained the situation. She reminded Olodumare that it was the women who brought life, love, and balance to the world. Without the divine feminine, the world could not survive.

Olodumare listened, and balance was restored. The rivers flowed again, and life returned to the Earth. This story shows how Oshun fights injustice not with violence, but with wisdom and truth. She teaches us that even when others try to silence us, we can still stand in our power.

Strength in Softness

Many people misunderstand what it means to be strong. They think strength is about being loud, hard, or angry. Oshun shows us another way.

Her strength lies in her softness. She chooses kindness, not because she is weak, but because she understands its power. She listens deeply, loves openly, and still protects herself when needed. She knows when to speak and when to remain silent. She knows how to forgive, but also how to stand firm when someone crosses a line.

In one myth, the orishas were in a disagreement. Shango, the orisha of thunder, was ready to solve the problem with fire and force. Ogun, the orisha of iron, wanted to cut through the conflict. But Oshun stepped in with a gentle voice and a clever plan. She offered honey to the orishas, reminding them of sweetness, unity, and peace.

Her plan worked. The orishas calmed down and reached an agreement. Once again, Oshun used her emotional strength to solve a problem that others thought required force.

This is one of her greatest lessons: softness is not the opposite of strength; it is a different kind of strength. It is the power to heal wounds, build trust, and create lasting peace.

Emotional Intelligence: Oshun's Quiet Superpower

Oshun is deeply connected to the emotions of others. She understands pain, love, jealousy, joy, fear, and hope. She doesn't hide her feelings, and she doesn't expect others to either. Instead, she teaches that emotions are messages from the soul. If we learn to listen, we can make better choices and grow stronger.

This type of wisdom is known as emotional intelligence. It means:

- Knowing how you feel and why.
- Understanding how others feel.
- Communicating clearly without hurting others.
- Making decisions with both the heart and the mind.

Oshun is a master of this. She knows when to comfort and when to correct. She listens with patience but also tells the truth when needed. She reminds us that it is okay to feel everything. Still, we must also learn to manage those feelings with care and consideration.

If you ever feel overwhelmed by emotions, imagine Oshun standing beside a river, holding a mirror and a fan. The mirror reflects truth, and the fan cools the heat of strong emotions. With her guidance, you can learn to honor your feelings without letting them control you.

Boundaries Are Sacred

One of the most important lessons Oshun teaches is about boundaries.

As the goddess of love, she is open-hearted and generous. But she is not a doormat. When people try to take advantage of her kindness, she doesn't just smile and take it. She speaks up. She walks away. She sets clear limits.

There is a story of a man who kept asking Oshun for help but never gave anything in return, not thanks, not respect, not even a kind word. He thought Oshun's giving nature meant he could ask for more and more. One day, Oshun stopped answering his prayers. She withdrew her energy, and he realized he had lost something precious.

Oshun's lesson here is clear: giving is a gift, not an obligation. True love includes balance. We must give and receive with respect. If someone crosses your boundaries again and again, you have every right to protect your peace.

Setting boundaries does not mean being mean. It means being honest about what you can give and what you will not accept. Oshun reminds us that self-respect is a key part of love.

Discernment: Seeing What Others Cannot

Another gift Oshun holds is discernment, the ability to see beneath the surface. She doesn't just listen to what people say; she feels their energy, watches their actions, and trusts her intuition.

In many myths, Oshun sees things that others miss. She knows when someone is lying, even if their words sound sweet. She can sense when a situation is off, even if it appears to be going well on the outside. This ability to read between the lines is a testament to her deep wisdom.

She teaches us to trust our inner voice. If something feels wrong, pay attention. If someone's actions don't match their words, believe the actions. If your heart is uneasy, listen to it.

Discernment helps us make smarter choices. It keeps us safe from harm and helps us choose the right people to trust. Oshun shows us that wisdom is not just knowledge; it's the ability to feel the truth and act on it.

The Fire Within Oshun

Although she is often associated with water, Oshun also holds fire within her spirit. When needed, she can become fierce, bold, and unstoppable. She is not afraid to defend what matters or to call out injustice when she sees it.

In one legend, when Ogun, the orisha of iron, became angry and went into the forest, the other orishas could not bring him back. The world needed his tools, his fire, his strength. Without him, work and progress came to a halt.

Oshun was the only one who could calm him. She entered the forest not with fear, but with a mix of grace and fire. She spoke his language, danced with confidence, and reminded him of his purpose. She used her own powerful energy, not to fight, but to guide.

This story shows her boldness. She does not let fear hold her back. When others step back, she steps forward. Her fire comes from love, but it burns away lies, fear, and injustice.

Resilience: Rising Again and Again

Life is not always easy. Even Oshun has faced loss, rejection, and pain. But she always rises again. This is what we call resilience, the ability to keep going after being knocked down.

One of the most touching myths about Oshun speaks of her tears. When she was ignored by the other orishas, she felt heartbroken. She cried, and her tears became the rivers of the Earth. Instead of letting pain destroy her, she transformed it into something beautiful.

Her rivers now flow through cities and forests. They bring water, life, and healing. Every drop reminds us that even our sorrow can lead to something powerful.

Oshun teaches that it is okay to cry. It is okay to feel hurt. But don't stay in the pain forever. Let it shape you, not break you. Like Oshun, we can turn tears into rivers that flow with strength.

Oshun's Wisdom in Everyday Life

So, how can we bring Oshun's wisdom into our daily lives? Here are some simple ways:

Speak with Intention

Oshun chooses her words carefully. Practice speaking in a way that is kind, honest, and clear. Don't gossip or spread harm. Use your voice to uplift and solve problems.

Create a Justice Journal

When you feel someone has mistreated you, write about it. Ask yourself: What do I need? What do I deserve? What would Oshun do in this situation?

This helps you sort through feelings and plan your next steps with confidence.

Practice Mirror Wisdom

Each morning, look into a mirror and ask:

- What do I feel today?
- What do I need?
- How can I protect my peace?

Over time, this practice builds emotional intelligence and self-trust.

Honor Your Boundaries

If someone crosses a line, speak up calmly and respectfully. Say, *"That doesn't feel right to me,"* or *"I need space."* Oshun wants you to protect your spirit with grace and courage.

8

EMOTIONAL AND SPIRITUAL RENEWAL FROM OSHUN THE HEALER

OSHUN IS WELL KNOWN AS A GODDESS OF LOVE, BEAUTY, AND abundance. But one of her most powerful gifts is her ability to heal. She is a sacred force who brings comfort in times of pain, hope when we feel lost, and peace when our hearts are broken. She doesn't just heal physical illness; she helps us restore balance in our emotions and spirit.

Throughout her stories and in the traditions of her worshipers, Oshun appears during moments of sadness, heartbreak, and spiritual confusion. She brings light when things feel dark. She reminds us that healing isn't about pretending to be okay, it's about slowly coming back to life after being hurt.

In this chapter, we'll explore how Oshun helps with emotional wounds. You'll learn about rituals with water and honey, healing prayers, and the deeper lesson of Oshun's energy: you are not broken, you are becoming.

Oshun's Presence in Times of Grief

Grief comes in many forms. It may be the loss of a loved one, the end of a relationship, or even losing a dream you once held dear.

When we are grieving, it can feel like we are underwater, heavy, and unable to breathe. This is when Oshun's healing power becomes especially important.

Oshun, as the goddess of rivers, understands what it means to flow through sorrow. Her own myths speak of moments when she cried, when she was ignored, or when her love was not returned. But even in those painful times, she found a way to keep going, and she used her pain to bring life back to the world.

When you are in grief, Oshun's energy surrounds you with compassion. She does not rush you. She sits beside you. She allows your tears. In fact, she welcomes them because she knows that every tear carries emotion that needs to be released. Healing begins when we allow ourselves to feel.

You can call on Oshun during these moments by speaking to her near a body of water or through a simple prayer. You might say:

"Oshun, mother of sweet waters, help me carry this grief. Let your river wash my sorrow, and let me find peace again.

Ashe."

Healing from Heartbreak

Heartbreak can be just as painful as physical injury. Whether it's from a breakup, betrayal, or deep disappointment, it leaves an ache that feels hard to heal. Oshun, as a goddess of love, understands this kind of pain very well.

In many of her stories, Oshun loves deeply. But she is not immune to heartbreak. There are tales where she is misunderstood, left behind, or not taken seriously. Still, she never gives up on herself. She reminds us that even when love ends or changes, we are still whole.

One of the ways Oshun teaches us to heal is through self-love. When others do not give us the love we need, she invites us to give it to ourselves. She encourages us to look in the mirror, not to focus on our appearance, but to see our strength, value, and beauty from within.

A simple mirror ritual you can try is this:

1. Stand in front of a mirror with a yellow candle lit beside you.
2. Hold a small bowl of honey in your hand.

Say: *"Oshun, help me see the sweetness in myself. Help me love who I am."*

3. Dip a finger in the honey and taste it. Let that sweetness remind you of your worth.

You are not defined by who left or who hurt you. You are defined by how deeply you return to yourself.

Oshun and Emotional Balance

Sometimes we don't know exactly what's wrong. We just feel off. Maybe we're anxious, tired, or constantly upset. These emotional imbalances can build over time. And if we don't take care of them, they can block us from feeling joy.

Oshun's energy teaches that emotions are like water, they must move. If we hold in sadness, anger, or fear, they get stuck. However, if we allow them to flow through healthy actions, such as crying, writing, praying, or dancing, we create space for healing.

Water is Oshun's sacred element for a reason. It reflects emotions, carries memory, and brings change. If you ever feel emotionally overwhelmed, consider taking an Oshun-inspired cleansing bath:

The Oshun Emotional Healing Bath Ritual

What You'll Need:

- A tub or a large bowl of clean water
- A few drops of honey
- Yellow or orange flower petals (such as marigold or sunflower)
- Cinnamon or a slice of orange
- A yellow candle

Steps:

1. Fill the tub with warm water.
2. Add the honey, petals, and cinnamon or orange to the water.
3. Light the yellow candle nearby.
4. Get in the water (or place your hands in the bowl if using a basin).

Say:

"Oshun, healer of hearts, wash away what weighs me down. Let your waters cleanse my spirit. Bring joy back to my soul. Ashe."

Soak or sit in silence for several minutes. Imagine the water pulling away stress and sadness.

When you leave the water, thank Oshun for her guidance. Allow yourself to rest. Healing takes time, and this ritual helps remind your spirit that you are safe, loved, and supported.

The Power of Honey in Healing

Honey is one of Oshun's most beloved offerings. It represents sweetness, comfort, and nourishment. But honey is more than just a treat; it has been used in healing for centuries. It soothes wounds, softens the heart, and brings warmth to cold spaces.

When you feel emotionally numb or distant, honey can help reconnect you with joy. It reminds you that even after pain, sweetness can return.

Here's a simple honey ritual for healing heavy emotions:

Ritual: Sweetness for the Spirit

What You'll Need:

- A spoonful of honey
- A quiet space
- A journal or piece of paper

Steps:

1. Sit in a quiet place with the honey in front of you.
2. Take a few deep breaths. Think about what you've been carrying lately, sadness, fear, guilt, loneliness.
3. Dip your finger into the honey. Taste it slowly.

Say aloud:

"Oshun, remind me that sweetness is still possible. Bring light to the parts of me that feel dark."

1. Write down one small thing that brings you joy or peace. It can be as simple as sunlight, a hug, or your favorite music.

2. Keep that note where you can see it. Let it remind you that healing comes one sweet moment at a time.

Letting Go to Make Space

Oshun's rivers are always flowing. They never stay in one place for long. In the same way, she teaches us to let go of what no longer serves us, old anger, past relationships, negative thoughts, so that we can move forward.

Letting go doesn't mean forgetting or pretending something didn't happen. It means releasing the hold it has on your heart. It's about choosing peace over pain, one step at a time.

Here's a practice for letting go:

Ritual: River Release

What You'll Need:

- A small bowl of water
- A stone or leaf
- A quiet place outdoors (or by a window)

Steps:

1. Hold the stone or leaf and think about something you need to release.
2. Speak to it:

"You were part of my path, but I no longer need you. I release you to Oshun's river. I make space for peace."

1. Drop the object into the bowl of water or into a river or stream if you are outside.

2. Watch it float or sink. Breathe deeply and let yourself feel the shift.

Even simple actions like this can help you feel lighter, clearer, and freer.

Renewal as a Spiritual Journey

Healing is not just about getting better, it's about becoming new. Oshun's healing doesn't return you to who you were before the pain. Instead, it helps you step into who you are becoming. This is the gift of spiritual renewal.

In the Osun-Osogbo Sacred Grove in Nigeria, people gather every year to honor Oshun at the river. They sing, dance, and offer thanks. Many come seeking healing. They don't just want relief; they want to reconnect with their purpose, their strength, and their joy.

This celebration reminds us that healing is not just a personal matter. It's also community work. When one person heals, they help others do the same. Oshun's energy brings people together through love, music, movement, and prayer.

You can create your own renewal celebration at home. It can be simple, light a candle, play uplifting music, and dance. Or write yourself a letter of hope for the future. These small acts are sacred steps toward joy.

Emotional Healing and the Sacred Feminine

Oshun is closely linked to feminine energy. But this doesn't only mean women; feminine energy is a part of all humans. It's the energy of feeling, nurturing, flowing, and creating. When we embrace our emotions, take time to rest, and honor beauty and care, we are connecting with this sacred force.

Oshun teaches us to love ourselves through all phases of life. Whether we feel powerful or broken, full or empty, she says, *"You are still worthy. You are still whole."*

Healing is a return to that truth.

Oshun's rivers never rush. They move at their own pace, winding through land, touching all they pass, bringing life wherever they go. Your healing is like that river.

You don't have to rush.

You don't have to *"get over it."*

You just have to keep flowing.

Oshun walks with you through every step of your journey, through your tears, through your silence, through your laughter. Her hands are gentle but strong. Her voice is soft but wise.

She reminds you that healing is not about becoming perfect. It's about returning to yourself with more love than ever before.

So breathe deeply. Speak kindly to your heart. Taste something sweet. Sit near water. And know that you are healing, even now.

9
FERTILITY, BIRTH, AND WOMEN'S WELLNESS

OSHUN IS A GODDESS WHO GIVES LIFE. SHE IS DEEPLY CONNECTED to fertility, childbirth, and the health of women and families. In the Yoruba tradition, and across the African Diaspora, Oshun is seen as a protector of women's bodies and their sacred power to bring life into the world.

But Oshun's gifts go beyond the physical act of creating a child. She also inspires emotional and creative fertility, helping people give birth to new ideas, new dreams, and new ways of living. Her energy reminds us that fertility is not just about having babies; it's about the ability to grow, renew, and nourish something from within.

In this chapter, we will explore Oshun's role in women's wellness, from healing the womb to encouraging emotional and spiritual growth. We will also learn about rituals for conception, pregnancy, and feminine cycles, and how Oshun supports women through each stage of life.

Oshun as the Guardian of Fertility

In Yoruba belief, Oshun is one of the most powerful Orishas connected to reproduction and fertility. She watches over the womb, the menstrual cycle, and the delicate balance that allows a person to bring life into the world. For centuries, women and families have prayed to her for help with conception, healthy pregnancies, and safe births.

In traditional stories, Oshun is often the only Orisha who knows how to create and sustain life. There's a famous tale where the other Orishas try to build the Earth but fail. They ignore Oshun, thinking she's only good for love and beauty. But nothing grows without her. The rivers run dry, crops wither, and women are unable to give birth. Only when Oshun is called and honored does life begin to flourish.

This story teaches that true power lies in creation and that Oshun holds the key to that power.

Women Healed by Her Waters

Many myths and personal stories tell of women who were blessed by Oshun's healing energy after struggling with fertility. In one well-known tale, a woman who was unable to conceive made a journey to Oshun's sacred river. She brought honey, oranges, and yellow flowers. She knelt at the riverbank, poured water over herself, and prayed with her whole heart.

Moved by the woman's devotion, Oshun appeared in a vision. She told the woman to hold on to her faith and to treat her body with care and love. Within a year, the woman became pregnant. Her child was seen as a gift from Oshun.

In today's world, many still visit rivers to ask Oshun for help with pregnancy. Others may do it symbolically, in their own home or during meditation. The key is connection, Oshun responds when she is approached with honesty, love, and respect.

Ritual for Conception

When a person is trying to conceive, it can evoke a range of emotions, hope, worry, excitement, and fear. This ritual honors both the physical and emotional aspects of that journey.

What You'll Need:

- A small bowl of clean water
- A spoonful of honey
- A yellow candle
- Yellow flowers (like marigolds or sunflowers)
- A quiet space

Steps:

1. Create a peaceful space, either at an altar or near a window, to enhance your meditation experience.
2. Place the water, honey, flowers, and candle together.
3. Light the candle and sit comfortably.
4. Dip your finger in the honey, taste it, and say:

"Oshun, sweet mother of life, bless my body and spirit. Make me ready to receive, to hold, and to carry new life. Ashe."

1. Touch a few drops of water to your lower belly. Imagine Oshun's golden energy filling your womb or creative center with light.
2. Close the ritual by offering thanks, and keep the flowers near your bed for three days.

This ritual is not only for physical pregnancy, it can also be used when you are preparing to create something new, like a project or a dream.

Oshun and the Sacred Womb

Oshun teaches that the womb is not just a place of birth; it is a center of power and energy. Even for those who do not wish to have children or cannot, the womb still holds creative energy, deep intuition, and emotional wisdom.

In many African traditions, the womb is honored as the seat of life. Maintaining a healthy lifestyle means more than just caring for your body, it also involves nurturing your thoughts, relationships, and emotional well-being. Oshun invites women to honor their wombs with love and attention, especially during their menstrual cycle.

Ritual for Menstrual Cycle and Womb Healing

Instead of seeing your period as a burden, Oshun encourages you to view it as a time of renewal and inner power.

What You'll Need:

- A warm bath or foot soak
- Yellow or white cloth
- Lavender or rose oil
- A journal

Steps:

1. Soak in warm water, breathing deeply and relaxing your body.
2. Afterward, wrap yourself in the yellow or white cloth.
3. Sit quietly and write in your journal:
   ○ What am I letting go of this cycle?

○ What am I ready to call in?

4. Light a candle and say:

"Oshun, keeper of my sacred rhythms, guide me through this cycle with peace and strength."

You can do this ritual monthly, or whenever you need to reconnect with your inner rhythm.

Supporting Healthy Pregnancies

Pregnancy is a sacred time marked by profound transformation. Oshun is often called upon during this time to protect the baby, ease discomfort, and bring peace to the parent. Devotees may wear yellow, visit rivers, or keep an Oshun statue nearby.

Prayers to Oshun during pregnancy may include:

"Oshun, golden river, keep me and this child safe. Wrap us in your joy and let your waters protect us."

Some also place offerings of oranges, honey, or cinnamon near their bedside, asking Oshun to bring ease during labor.

Ritual for Birth and Safe Delivery

This ritual can be performed in the final weeks of pregnancy or by loved ones who are praying for someone who is expecting.

What You'll Need:

- A yellow cloth or scarf
- A piece of gold jewelry
- A small bowl of water

Steps:

1. Place the cloth on a flat surface with the jewelry in the center.
2. Pour water into the bowl and set it on the cloth.
3. Say aloud:

"Oshun, mother of rivers, bless this birth with strength, joy, and light. Let the child arrive safely and the parent be well. Ashe."

1. Leave the setup in a peaceful place until after birth, and then return the water to a natural space (like a garden or tree base).

Motherhood and Emotional Wellness

Oshun not only protects the physical body during childbirth, but she also nurtures the heart. Motherhood can bring exhaustion, confusion, and deep emotion. It is not always easy. But Oshun reminds mothers that they are not alone. They are held. They are seen.

If you are a mother feeling overwhelmed, Oshun's guidance is simple: slow down, drink water, and speak kindly to yourself. Being a parent is sacred, but it's also human. You are allowed to ask for help. You are allowed to rest.

Emotional Fertility and Creative Energy

Fertility is not just about babies. It is about being open to life. Oshun teaches us that creating beauty, joy, or change is just as sacred as creating a child.

Have you ever had a big dream that scared you? Or a project you wanted to start but didn't know how? That's creative fertility at work. Oshun whispers: *"Yes, you can."*

Even during times when physical fertility is not possible, because of age, health, or choice, you can still honor your creative energy. You can paint, write, sing, garden, cook, or start something new. That's Oshun moving through you.

Ritual for Creative Renewal

This ritual is for anyone who feels stuck or unsure. It helps open the creative channel and invites Oshun's support.

What You'll Need:

- A yellow candle
- A small mirror
- A glass of water
- A notebook or sketchpad

Steps:

1. Light the candle and place the mirror in front of you.
2. Look into the mirror and say:

"Oshun, awaken the creator in me. Let me birth something beautiful."

1. Take a sip of the water, feeling it move through you.
2. Begin writing or drawing, don't worry about the result. Just let your ideas flow.
3. Close with thanks, and leave the candle burning (safely) for a few minutes longer.

Oshun's Message to All Women

Whether or not you ever give birth, Oshun sees you as a sacred vessel. Your body is wise. Your heart is strong. Your dreams are important.

She asks you to listen to your needs, to your intuition, to your longings. She reminds you that you deserve care, pleasure, and support. Your cycle, your voice, your softness, your fire, it's all divine.

When we trust ourselves and take time to care for our health, we are honoring Oshun.

Caring for the Feminine in All People

Although this chapter focuses on women's wellness, it's important to remember that everyone carries both masculine and feminine energy. Some people assigned male at birth may also feel a deep connection to Oshun's nurturing and healing energy. Some women may not feel connected to traditional roles, but they still possess creative and emotional power.

Oshun welcomes all who come with sincerity and respect. Her energy is for anyone who wants to create, heal, and grow.

If you are reading this while hoping for a child, caring for your womb, creating something new, or learning to love your body, Oshun is with you. Her river flows through every part of your journey.

She says:

"You are the garden. You are the seed. You are the rain. And you are the sun. All you need is already inside you. Trust the flow."

May her waters bless your body, may her light guide your dreams, and may your life bloom in many beautiful ways.

Ashe.

10

OSHUN'S ABUNDANT PATH OF PROSPERITY

OSHUN IS WELL KNOWN AS THE GODDESS OF RIVERS, LOVE, AND beauty, but she is also deeply connected to abundance. Her energy flows through everything that brings sweetness to life, love, joy, health, and wealth. On her golden path, Oshun teaches us that true prosperity is more than just financial gain. It includes peace of mind, purpose, strong relationships, and the courage to follow our dreams.

In this chapter, we'll explore how Oshun supports abundance on all levels. We'll also learn how to attract blessings through rituals, gratitude, and spiritual alignment. Finally, we'll look at the importance of staying grounded and honest when working with Oshun's energy of wealth.

Let's begin by understanding what abundance really means.

What Is Abundance?

Many people think of abundance as having a lot of money or material possessions. While that's part of it, Oshun teaches a deeper truth. Abundance is a state of being. It means feeling full, satisfied, joyful, and in sync with life's flow.

You can be financially rich and still feel empty or fearful. You can also have very little and still feel peaceful and thankful. Abundance comes when your heart and soul are open, and when you live in a way that honors your gifts and purpose.

Oshun's rivers show us that abundance is about flow. When water moves freely, it nourishes everything it touches. But when it's blocked, it becomes still, heavy, or dry. The same is true for our energy, time, and money. We are most prosperous when we allow things to move, giving, receiving, and trusting the process.

Oshun's Symbols of Wealth and Joy

Many of Oshun's sacred items are connected to prosperity. Gold, honey, oranges, and mirrors are not just beautiful, they carry deep spiritual meaning.

- Gold represents wealth, beauty, and sacred value. It reminds us that we are worthy of abundance.
- Honey brings sweetness and joy. Oshun uses it to attract blessings and soften challenges.
- Oranges and citrus fruits symbolize health, energy, and fruitfulness.
- Mirrors reflect self-love. They help us recognize our own light and feel confident in ourselves.

When we honor these symbols with respect, we open ourselves to the blessings Oshun wants to give.

The Spiritual Meaning of Wealth

Oshun teaches that wealth is not only for personal gain, it's also for sharing. When we utilize our resources to care for ourselves and others, we cultivate stronger, more fulfilling lives. Oshun's energy reminds us that true wealth includes kindness, creativity, and connection.

Wealth that flows with honesty and gratitude becomes a blessing. But when people chase riches out of fear, greed, or pride, they often feel lost, even when they "have it all." Oshun reminds us that prosperity with peace is the ultimate goal, not just more money.

Aligning with Oshun's Abundance

Suppose you want to invite Oshun's energy of prosperity into your life. In that case, the first step is to be thankful for what you already have. Gratitude is like a magnet, it pulls more blessings toward you. When you focus only on what's missing, you block the flow.

Here are a few ways to align with Oshun's abundant path:

Practice Daily Gratitude

Each day, write down three things you're thankful for. They can be small, like a smile from a friend or a warm cup of tea. Over time, this simple habit changes your energy and helps you see the abundance already around you.

Keep Your Energy Moving

Don't hold onto money, time, or emotions so tightly that you become stuck. Give when you can. Be open to receive. Allow joy and generosity to flow.

Follow Your Joy

Oshun supports what makes you feel alive. Whether it's dancing, cooking, writing, or helping others, do more of what lights you up. That's where abundance lives.

Care for Your Appearance and Space

Keep your home and body in a state of care and beauty. Oshun values elegance and grace, not to impress others, but to honor yourself.

Ritual for Financial Abundance

This ritual helps you invite Oshun's energy into your financial life. It can be done at any time, but Fridays (Oshun's sacred day) are especially powerful.

What You'll Need:

- A gold or yellow candle
- A bowl of honey
- Five coins (clean and shiny)
- A glass of clean water
- A piece of yellow paper and a pen

Steps:

1. Set up a small altar or clean space.
2. Place the candle in the center, with the honey, coins, and water around it.
3. On the yellow paper, write your name and a clear, honest statement about your desire (for example, *"I welcome financial opportunities that help me grow and give."*).
4. Light the candle. Speak this prayer:

"Oshun, golden mother of abundance, let your rivers flow into my life. Bless me with prosperity, joy, and purpose. I open my hands and my heart to receive. Ashe."

1. Touch each coin to the honey, and then place them in front of the candle.

2. Drink a sip of water, imagining your spirit being refreshed.
3. Let the candle burn safely, and leave the setup for at least one full day.

Later, you can spend or donate the coins with intention, releasing the energy into the world.

Ritual for Creative Prosperity

Oshun supports not only money, but also creative success. This ritual is designed for artists, entrepreneurs, or anyone seeking clarity and growth in their professional endeavors.

What You'll Need:

- A yellow scarf or cloth
- Cinnamon or a sweet perfume
- A mirror
- A journal or sketchbook

Steps:

1. Sit in front of the mirror with the scarf over your shoulders.
2. Lightly dab the cinnamon or perfume on your wrists and neck.
3. Look into the mirror and say:

"Oshun, bringer of beauty and ideas, flow through me. Let my gifts shine bright."

1. Spend 15–20 minutes writing, drawing, or planning your creative dream.

2. Close with thanks. Wrap the scarf and journal together and keep them near your altar or bedside.

Doing this regularly helps keep your energy inspired and focused.

Building a Prosperity Altar

A home altar is a beautiful way to stay connected to Oshun's energy. You can create one to honor her and support your intention for abundance.

Items to Include:

- Yellow or gold cloth
- A mirror
- A bowl of honey
- Fresh flowers (especially yellow or orange)
- Small coins or jewelry
- A photo or image of Oshun
- A cup of clean water

Keep your altar clean, fresh, and joyful. Visit it daily, even for just a minute, to express gratitude, set intentions, or seek guidance.

Integrity in Manifesting Wealth

While it's wonderful to welcome more money or success, it's important to do so with spiritual integrity. Oshun does not bless dishonest paths. She rewards those who walk with grace, patience, and care for others.

Here are a few ways to stay in alignment:

- Don't compare your journey to others. Your blessings are unique to you.
- Don't try to rush or force results. Prosperity grows best when it flows naturally.

- Don't seek wealth just for ego or control. Ask: *"How will my blessings help others, too?"*

When your intentions are pure, Oshun will guide you. However, if you attempt to manipulate her or exploit her name for personal gain, her energy may withdraw.

A Word on Generosity

One of the best ways to stay connected to Oshun's abundant path is through giving. This doesn't mean giving away everything, or giving when it hurts, but it means sharing from the heart when you can.

This might be:

- Donating to a cause
- Helping a friend without expecting anything back
- Giving compliments or emotional support
- Offering your talents or time to uplift someone

Giving creates a cycle. What flows out with love often returns multiplied.

Signs of Prosperity From Oshun

As you align with Oshun's energy, you may begin to notice little signs that she's with you. These are often gentle, joyful, or golden in nature.

Watch for:

- Finding coins or gold-colored objects in surprising places
- Seeing peacocks, bees, or butterflies
- Hearing flowing water or dreaming of rivers
- Feeling drawn to the color yellow or gold
- Moments of sudden joy, laughter, or beauty

These signs remind you to trust, to stay open, and to keep your heart grateful.

Daily Affirmations for Prosperity

You can say these affirmations each morning or during ritual:

- *"I am worthy of wealth, joy, and success."*
- *"Abundance flows to me with ease and grace."*
- *"I honor Oshun by walking in light and love."*
- *"My heart is open, and I receive with gratitude."*
- *"I share my gifts freely and trust in the flow."*

Writing them down and placing them near your altar or mirror can deepen their power.

Prosperity and Life Purpose

Sometimes, people ask: "How do I know if I'm doing what I'm meant to do?" Oshun's answer is simple: follow your joy.

When you are doing something that brings you to life, something that helps others, uses your gifts, and makes you feel alive; you are on the right path. And that path will often lead to both emotional and financial prosperity.

If you're unsure where to start, ask Oshun for guidance. Sit by water, light a yellow candle, and speak from your heart. Her answers may come as feelings, dreams, or quiet knowing.

Oshun is not a goddess of greed. She is a goddess of grace. Her rivers do not flood just to impress. They flow to give life. Her gold does not shine for power; it glows to remind us of beauty, purpose, and joy.

To walk Oshun's abundant path, remember this:

- Be thankful for what you have.
- Give freely and joyfully.
- Ask with honesty.
- Trust the flow.
- Stay open to receive.

You are worthy of good things. You are allowed to dream big. With Oshun beside you, may your heart be full, your table be rich, and your life overflow with blessings.

Ashe.

11

RITUALS, OFFERINGS, AND DAILY PRACTICES

WORKING WITH OSHUN IS ABOUT MORE THAN BELIEF; IT'S ABOUT building a relationship. Just like any relationship, it grows stronger over time, with attention and love. One of the best ways to connect with Oshun is by creating a sacred routine. Through rituals, offerings, and daily practices, you can invite her energy into your life and keep it flowing with intention.

This chapter serves as a guide to help you form a meaningful and personal spiritual connection with Oshun. Whether you're new to her or have been walking with her for years, these practices will support your journey.

Why Rituals Matter

Rituals are a way of showing respect, love, and devotion. They help us focus, slow down, and connect with something greater than ourselves. When we create rituals for Oshun, we're not just "doing tasks." We're building spiritual bridges.

Oshun is drawn to beauty, sweetness, and sincerity. She responds when we offer with open hearts and clear intentions. Your ritual doesn't have to be perfect. It just needs to be real.

Creating a Sacred Routine with Oshun

A spiritual routine doesn't need to be long or complicated. It can be as little as a few minutes each day, a weekly offering, or a monthly ritual. What matters is consistency and honesty. Here are some ways to incorporate Oshun into your daily routine.

Morning Gratitude

Start each morning by saying *"Thank you, Oshun."* You can say this before getting out of bed, while brushing your teeth, or when lighting a candle. It's a simple way to invite her energy into your day.

Candle Work

Lighting a yellow or gold candle is one of the most common ways to honor Oshun. You can light it while praying, journaling, or just sitting quietly. The flame represents light, warmth, and connection.

Weekly Offerings

Pick one day each week, Friday is best, as it's Oshun's sacred day, and make a small offering. You might place flowers on your altar or pour a bit of honey into a bowl. Even simple acts, when done with love, carry deep meaning.

Reflective Journaling

Write letters to Oshun in your journal. Share your dreams, worries, or prayers. Over time, you may start to feel her presence in your words or thoughts. You may receive guidance this way.

Offerings for Oshun

Offerings are gifts. They show respect and love while helping you align with Oshun's energy. Here are some of the most common offerings used to honor her:

Honey

Sweet and golden, honey is one of Oshun's favorite offerings. It symbolizes love, joy, and healing. Always taste the honey before offering it to her. In some traditions, this honors a time when Oshun's honey was poisoned, and she learned to test it first to ensure its purity.

You can offer honey in a small glass bowl on your altar or pour a little into river water during rituals.

Oranges and Citrus Fruits

These bright, juicy fruits reflect Oshun's vitality. Oranges are especially sacred. You can place five oranges on her altar, peel one and float it in water, or squeeze the juice as part of a ritual bath.

Sweets and Pastries

Oshun enjoys desserts that bring joy and celebration. Small cakes, cookies, or candy can be placed as offerings. Choose sweets you would enjoy yourself, Oshun appreciates generosity.

Flowers

Fresh flowers, especially those with a yellow hue like sunflowers or marigolds, honor Oshun's beauty and grace. You can place them in a vase on your altar or float them in water as part of an offering.

Cinnamon and Spices

Cinnamon is a warming spice associated with Oshun's fiery and passionate side. Sprinkle it around candles, include it in spiritual baths, or place a cinnamon stick in your offering bowl.

Types of Rituals

Different moments call for different rituals. Some are quiet and personal. Others are more formal or connected to natural cycles. Below are some powerful ritual types for working with Oshun.

New Moon Ritual for Fresh Beginnings

The new moon is a time for starting over, setting intentions, and calling in blessings. Oshun's energy fits beautifully with new moon magic.

You'll Need:

- Yellow candle
- Bowl of water with five drops of honey
- Paper and pen
- A flower (yellow or white)

Steps:

1. Clean your space. Sit quietly and light the candle.
2. Write down what you want to attract (love, joy, clarity, etc.).
3. Place the paper under the bowl of water.
4. Dip your fingers into the water and touch your heart.
5. Say:

"Oshun, I welcome your golden light. Guide me into this new cycle. May my wishes flow like your river. Ashe."

1. Float the flower in the bowl. Let the candle burn safely.
2. After the ritual, pour the water into the Earth or a natural body of water.

River Offering

Oshun is the goddess of rivers. Taking offerings to the water is one of the most sacred ways to honor her.

Best Offerings for the River:

- Oranges
- Flowers
- Honey (in biodegradable containers)
- Written prayers (on natural paper)

How to Do It:

- Visit a clean river, stream, or even a small creek.
- Speak your prayer aloud or silently from your heart.
- Offer your items to the river with gratitude.
- Spend time in silence, feeling Oshun's presence through the water.

If you don't live near a river, you can fill a bowl with clean water and use it as a symbolic river. Speak to the water, and then pour it into the Earth after your ritual.

Love Bath for Attraction and Self-Love

Oshun's baths are powerful tools for healing and drawing in positive energy.

You'll Need:

- A warm bath or a large bowl of water
- Five slices of orange
- A spoonful of honey
- Flower petals (yellow or white)
- A few drops of perfume or essential oil

Steps:

1. Mix all the ingredients into the water.
2. Step into the bath or pour the water over your body.
3. As you bathe, say:

"Oshun, bless me with your sweetness. May I glow with love and confidence. Ashe."

1. Visualize yourself surrounded by golden light.
2. After your bath, dress in something that makes you feel beautiful.

Do this on Fridays or when you need a boost of love and joy.

Daily Devotion Ideas

Not every ritual needs to be long. These daily devotion ideas are simple ways to keep Oshun close to you.

Light a Candle

Even a tea light candle can be powerful when lit with intention. Light it and say a few words of thanks. Let it remind you that Oshun is near.

Say a Prayer or Chant

Here's a short daily prayer you can use:

"Oshun, mother of sweetness and flow, guide me in love and grace. May my words be kind, my actions pure, and my heart open. Ashe."

Or use a simple chant like:

"Oshun, flow through me."

Say it while walking, meditating, or cleaning your space.

Journaling

Keep a special notebook for Oshun. Use it to:

- Write prayers or letters
- Record dreams and signs
- Track blessings and goals
- Reflect on your spiritual journey

Writing is a sacred act. Oshun often speaks through symbols, feelings, and sudden insight.

Sacred Time: Fridays with Oshun

Fridays are considered Oshun's day. Many devotees use this time to honor her with a fresh candle, a small ritual, or a special meal.

Friday Ideas:

- Wear yellow or gold clothing.
- Play music and dance in her honor.
- Cook something sweet and offer the first bite.
- Watch water flow, visit a fountain or take a mindful shower.

Using Friday as a regular "date" with Oshun helps you stay spiritually connected, even during busy weeks.

Working with Oshun Respectfully

While Oshun is warm and generous, she also expects to be respected. Here are a few reminders when working with her energy:

- Always approach her with honesty.

- Do not lie, brag, or make promises you don't plan to keep.
- Be mindful of how you handle offerings, don't waste or disrespect them.
- Never use her name to try to control others or get quick riches.

Oshun is a goddess of joy, but also of boundaries. Treat your relationship with her like a sacred friendship.

What If I Can't Do a Full Ritual?

That's okay. Oshun doesn't require perfection. You can honor her in small ways:

- Smile at someone who needs it.
- Pick up trash from a river or park.
- Take a moment of silence near water.
- Say *"Thank you"* when something good happens.

Every kind act, every grateful thought, is part of your offering.

Oshun's Presence in Everyday Life

Once you begin these practices, you may start to notice Oshun's signs around you. These are gentle reminders that she's near.

You might see:

- Coins on the ground
- A peacock feather or image
- Flowing water in dreams
- A sudden burst of joy or inspiration
- A sweet smell with no clear source

Pay attention to how you feel in those moments. Oshun often speaks through sensation, intuition, and natural beauty.

Rituals and offerings are more than "spells" or spiritual chores. They are gifts of time and heart. Through these practices, you are choosing to walk with Oshun, to learn from her, to receive from her, and to become more like her.

Whether it's through a bowl of honey, a quiet prayer, or a joyful dance, every offering you make strengthens the river between you and the divine. And with Oshun, that river is always golden.

So take your time. Be gentle with yourself. Let your devotion be real. And trust that when you honor Oshun with love, she will always find a way to bless you in return.

Ashe.

12

CREATING AND HONORING A SACRED ALTAR

AN ALTAR IS A SACRED SPACE. IT IS A QUIET PLACE WHERE YOUR spirit can meet with the divine. When you create an altar for Oshun, you are inviting her into your life in a real and physical way. It is like opening your heart and saying, *"Come sit with me."*

Altars are not just about decorations or religious objects. They are about connection. They help you stay focused, grounded, and aware of the spiritual world around you. With love and care, your Oshun altar can become a powerful tool for healing, joy, and transformation.

What Is an Altar?

An altar is a dedicated space for spiritual work. It can be a small shelf, a table, or even a corner of a windowsill. It holds the items you use to honor a spirit or divine energy. For Oshun, an altar becomes a sacred space filled with beauty, light, and intention.

Altars can be used for prayer, meditation, offerings, and reflection. They are also a way to build a closer relationship with the orisha you are honoring. In this case, your altar becomes a bridge between you and Oshun, a place where her energy can be felt and welcomed.

Oshun's Energy in the Altar

Oshun is the orisha of love, sweetness, beauty, rivers, and joy. She loves things that are bright, soft, and full of life. Your altar should reflect this. When selecting items for your altar, consider what brings you joy, peace, and gratitude. Think about the flow of water and the warmth of sunlight. Consider the combination of sweetness and softness, strength and elegance.

The more you fill your altar with intention and beauty, the more it will reflect Oshun's energy.

How to Build an Oshun Altar

You don't need a lot of money or fancy tools to create a sacred space. What you need is care, thoughtfulness, and honesty.

Step 1: Choose a Location

Select a quiet spot in your home where you can be undisturbed and focused. It could be a shelf in your room, a small table, or a private corner. Try to choose a spot that won't be disturbed by daily activity or clutter.

This space should feel calm and peaceful. It doesn't have to be perfect, but it should feel good to you.

Step 2: Cleanse the Space

Before setting up your altar, clean the space physically and spiritually. Dust the surface, then wipe it with water, and remove any debris that doesn't belong there.

To spiritually cleanse the space, you can:

- Burn sage, incense, or sweet herbs.
- Sprinkle water with a few drops of perfume or river water.
- Light a candle and say a simple prayer asking for the space to be blessed.

You might say:

"Oshun, may this space be pure and sweet, a place for your beauty and blessings. Ashe."

Step 3: Gather Your Altar Tools

Here are some traditional and symbolic items you may want to include:

- A yellow or gold cloth – This is the base of your altar. Oshun loves yellow and gold.
- A mirror – Mirrors represent self-reflection, beauty, and Oshun's wisdom.
- A bowl of honey – Honey stands for sweetness, healing, and love.
- Oranges or citrus fruits – These symbolize abundance and joy.
- Flowers – Yellow flowers, like sunflowers or marigolds, attract her energy.
- River water – This connects to her role as the goddess of rivers.
- Candles – Yellow, gold, or white candles can be lit during prayer.
- Small items of beauty – Jewelry, perfume, coins, or anything that shines and makes you feel happy.

You don't need every item listed above. Start with what you have. You can add more over time as you feel guided to do so.

Step 4: Arrange with Intention

When placing items on your altar, think about balance and beauty. Place the mirror in the center, the candle beside it, and the honey bowl in front. Arrange fruits and flowers around them. There's no single "right" way, follow your heart and let your creativity flow.

Just remember to treat the space with care. Every object should have a purpose and be placed with respect.

Seasonal vs. Permanent Altars

Some people create permanent altars that remain in place throughout the year. Others prefer to create temporary or seasonal altars that change with the moon cycle, special festivals, or times of need.

Permanent Altars

A permanent altar is a stable, ongoing relationship. It becomes a spiritual home that grows stronger the more you use it. It offers a space for daily prayer, offerings, and connection.

Pros:

- Easy to return to every day
- Gathers energy over time
- Strong sense of sacred space

Seasonal Altars

Seasonal or temporary altars help mark special occasions, full moons, or spiritual goals. You may create one when asking

Oshun for help with a specific issue, such as love, healing, or abundance.

Pros:

- Fresh and focused energy
- Useful for short-term intentions
- Can be set up outdoors or in different locations

You can even do both! Maintain a permanent altar and periodically refresh it with new items, colors, or symbols that align with your spiritual focus at the time.

Cleansing and Maintaining Your Altar

Once your altar is set up, it's important to care for it. Think of it like tending a beautiful garden. It doesn't need constant attention, but it does need love.

Weekly Care

Once a week, especially on Fridays:

- Dust the surface and items gently.
- Replace any wilted flowers or spoiled fruits.
- Refresh the honey if it's sticky or cloudy.
- Light a fresh candle and say a prayer.

You can also place crystals like citrine, amber, or rose quartz to boost the energy.

This weekly care keeps the altar spiritually clean and honors Oshun's love for freshness and beauty.

Seasonal Cleansing

With each new season or moon phase, you may want to:

- Rearrange items
- Add new offerings
- Rededicate the space with a special prayer

This helps your altar stay in tune with the natural cycles and your personal growth.

Inviting Oshun's Presence

Your altar is not just a decoration, it is a doorway. Through it, you invite Oshun's presence into your life. The more love and attention you offer, the more her energy will respond.

Here are ways to make Oshun feel welcomed:

Speak with Honesty

Talk to her as you would a wise and loving friend. You can say thank you, ask for help, or just speak from your heart.

Example:

"Oshun, I welcome your love and sweetness into this space. May it flow into my home and heart."

Offer Songs or Music

Oshun enjoys music, singing, and joyful sounds. Play soft music while lighting her candle. You might even sing to her, chant her name, or shake a rattle or bell.

Add Fragrance and Light

She is drawn to soft, sweet smells and soft light. Use perfume, incense, or scented oils like vanilla, rose, or orange blossom.

Candles, especially those with a gold or yellow hue, also help create a warm and inviting atmosphere.

Bring Your Joy

Oshun loves joy. Laugh, smile, and dance near your altar. When you're feeling happy, let her be part of it. You can even share sweets or a special meal with her.

A Simple Daily Altar Practice

Here's a basic routine you can do in just a few minutes:

1. Light a yellow candle.
2. Offer a fresh flower or a drop of honey.
3. Speak from your heart. Say what you're grateful for or what you need.
4. Sit in silence for one minute. Listen. Breathe.
5. Blow a kiss to Oshun or smile in her direction. Let her know you care.

This practice can change your whole day. It centers your heart and fills your space with peace.

Sample Prayer for the Altar

"Oshun, sweet river mother,

You who dance with golden light,

I offer you this space,

Full of beauty and truth.

May my life flow like your waters,

Soft, strong, and sacred.

Bless this altar.

Bless this heart.

Bless this home.

Ashe."

You can write your own prayers, too. The more personal, the better.

When You Can't Have an Altar

Sometimes you may not have the space, privacy, or freedom to build a full altar. That's okay. Oshun can still be honored.

Try these simple ideas:

- Keep a small yellow cloth in a drawer with a mirror and a tiny bottle of perfume.
- Carry a coin, an orange flower, or a river stone in your pocket.
- Create a "travel altar" in a small box or pouch.
- Use your phone background or lock screen as a digital altar, maybe a picture of a river, a golden flower, or an image of Oshun.

Remember, Oshun is everywhere. She flows through rivers, laughter, beauty, and love. The altar is just one way to welcome her in.

The Altar as a Living Relationship

Think of your altar as a friendship. It grows over time. On some days, you may feel deeply connected; on other days, you may feel quiet or distant. Both are okay.

Your job is to keep showing up with love, honesty, and care.

When you do, Oshun's energy will meet you there. She will come with blessings, insight, healing, and joy.

A well-loved altar becomes more than a table with objects; it becomes a sacred mirror of your own spiritual journey. It reflects your growth, your dreams, and your devotion.

And in return, it reflects the sweetness of Oshun back to you.

STORIES OF CONNECTION AND MIRACLES FROM DEVOTEE VOICES

OSHUN HAS TOUCHED THE LIVES OF COUNTLESS PEOPLE worldwide. From small moments of comfort to life-changing miracles, her energy moves through different cultures, languages, and walks of life. In this chapter, we listen to the real voices of those who call her mother, friend, healer, and guide.

These stories reveal that Oshun is more than a goddess of rivers and beauty; she is present in the daily struggles and small victories. She is the whisper in moments of doubt and the burst of joy in times of celebration. Each story is different, but all carry the golden thread of love, trust, and transformation.

Healing Through Water

Aisha, 33, Nigeria

I grew up in a village near the Osun River. As a child, I didn't understand why my grandmother always left offerings at the riverbank. She would walk there with flowers, honey, and songs, whispering prayers into the wind. I used to think it was just an old custom.

But when I was in my twenties, I faced something I couldn't ignore, deep sadness. I had lost my job, and my fiancé left me. I felt like everything in me had dried up. I couldn't eat, couldn't sleep, and my heart felt broken.

One morning, my grandmother told me, *"Oshun is waiting for you. Go to her."* I went to the river, unsure of what I was even doing. I brought honey and a yellow flower. I sat by the edge of the water and cried. I spoke to Oshun as if she were my sister, my mother, my friend.

As the tears flowed, something shifted. I felt lighter. The breeze wrapped around me like a hug. That was the first night I slept in weeks.

Over the next months, I returned again and again. Slowly, I healed. I found peace. Then, I was offered a new job, one that used my real talents. Today, I live with more joy than ever before. I still bring offerings to the river, and now I know why my grandmother did, too.

Love Returned

Carlos, 40, Cuba (Santería Practitioner)

In Santería, we call her Ochún. I was initiated in my late twenties, and from the beginning, I felt drawn to her. My padrino (godfather) told me she had chosen me for something special.

Years later, my wife and I were going through a rough time. We had grown apart. The love we had seemed lost. I prayed to Ochún. I gave her honey, lit her candle, and placed five oranges on her altar. I sang to her every Friday, asking her to help us find each other again.

Little by little, things changed. My wife began smiling again. We started spending time together, cooking, dancing like we used to.

One evening, she came to me and said, *"It feels like we're falling in love all over again."*

That was the moment I knew, Ochún had heard me. She doesn't always speak in a loud voice. Sometimes, it's a soft return, a slow healing of the heart.

Now, we go to the river as a family. We leave flowers and sweet things for her. My children call her Tía Ochún, Auntie Ochún. We don't just believe, we know.

A Dream and a Job

Monica, 27, United States

I didn't grow up religious. I didn't know anything about orishas. But after college, I couldn't find work. I was applying to jobs nonstop. Every rejection made me feel more hopeless. One night, I had a dream about a golden river. A woman in a yellow dress stood in the water. She was smiling and said, *"It's coming. Don't give up."*

I didn't know who she was. I googled "woman in a yellow dress in a river" and kept seeing pictures of Oshun. It gave me chills. I read everything I could. I bought a yellow candle and a small mirror. I placed them on a shelf in my room, along with a small bowl of honey.

Every day, I lit the candle and whispered, *"Thank you for being with me."*

Two weeks later, I was offered a job in a creative agency, my dream career. It was like everything suddenly fell into place. That yellow candle hasn't left my shelf since. I'm still learning, still growing, but I know now I'm not alone.

Comfort in Grief

Ana, 51, Brazil (Candomblé)

I lost my mother last year. She was my best friend. For weeks after her death, I couldn't feel anything but pain. My heart was heavy. In Candomblé, we honor Oxum for comfort, for healing, for sweetness when life turns bitter.

I went to my terreiro (temple) and asked our mãe-de-santo if I could prepare an offering. She helped me dress in yellow. We brought honey, cinnamon, and a golden necklace to the river near our city.

As I prayed, tears began to flow. But they weren't only sad tears. They were warm, as if I were being held. That night, I had a dream in which my mother was laughing. I woke up with the smell of oranges in the air.

Oxum gave me back the light inside me. She didn't take away the grief, but she helped me carry it with love. Now, when I think of my mother, I smile first before I cry.

A Teenage Awakening

Jayla, 16, USA

I don't tell many people about this, but Oshun changed my life.

I was really struggling with self-esteem. I didn't feel pretty. I didn't feel seen. Social media made me compare myself to everyone. I would cry at night and ask, *"What's wrong with me?"*

One day, I came across a post about Oshun. It said she's the goddess of beauty, but also of self-love and confidence. Something in me clicked. I started lighting a small candle each morning and saying one nice thing to myself.

I made a playlist of songs that made me feel powerful and danced in my room. I started smiling at myself in the mirror instead of picking myself apart. I even wrote *"You are golden"* on a sticky note and put it on my door.

Now, I feel like Oshun lives in my heart. She's not just about looks; she's about knowing you matter. I still have hard days, but I no longer hate myself. That's a miracle.

Crossing Cultures

Liam, 38, Ireland

I never thought I would connect to an African goddess. I was raised Catholic, and my spiritual journey has been full of twists. But while traveling in South America, I met a woman who practiced Santería. She spoke of Oshun with so much love. I was curious, so I looked into it further.

One day, while hiking alone, I stopped by a river and felt something... different. The sound of the water calmed me in a way I can't explain. I whispered a simple "thank you" to the sky.

Since then, I've worked with Oshun in my own way. I honor her in quiet rituals. I write poetry for her. I donate to women's shelters in her name. Though I live far from where her stories were born, I feel her in the water, in acts of kindness, in beauty.

Oshun crosses borders. She meets people wherever they are. You just have to open the door.

Mother and Midwife

Yemi, 45, Nigeria

I am a midwife. I deliver babies for a living, and every time, I call on Oshun.

I keep a yellow cloth in my birthing kit. I place honey on the mother's tongue if she is scared. I sing a quiet chant to Oshun when the baby is coming, asking her to bring sweetness and safe passage.

One time, a mother was struggling. The baby was not coming, and her pain was great. I whispered to Oshun, *"Please, help her."* Moments later, the mother relaxed. She cried out, and the baby came swiftly after.

It may sound small, but I know Oshun was there.

Oshun is with every woman in labor, every child entering the world. She is the song between heartbeats.

A River of Dreams

Camila, 22, Dominican Republic

I had never been to a real river before. I live in the city and had only seen them in pictures. But for months, I kept dreaming of one. A wide, golden river with soft singing voices in the background. A woman in white would stand there, offering me her hand, but I was afraid to go near.

After the fifth or sixth dream, I went to my grandmother. She told me, *"That is Oshun calling you."*

She took me to the countryside and led me to a real river. I stood in the water and felt something in me open up. I cried. I sang. I laughed. I felt alive again.

I now keep a picture of that river by my bed. I light a candle for Oshun once a week. She found me in my sleep, and now I meet her in my waking life.

Oshun in the City

Marcus, 30, Chicago

I'm a city guy. I work in tech, and my life is fast-paced. But I needed something spiritual. I was tired of feeling disconnected and drained.

A friend introduced me to the Orisha tradition. I learned about Oshun and felt drawn to her lightness. I built a tiny altar in my apartment, yellow cloth, a mirror, and a glass of water.

Each morning, I light a candle and thank her for the day. That small moment has changed everything. I approach my work with more peace. I listen better. I feel more generous.

Oshun brought flow into my life, not just in terms of money or success, but in how I navigate the world. Even in the middle of a busy city, I found my river.

One Last Blessing

Rosa, 72, Puerto Rico

I've walked with Oshun for many years. I've seen her bring love, peace, and healing. But my favorite moment was when my granddaughter was born.

My daughter had a hard pregnancy. The doctors said the baby might not make it. I went to the river every day. I brought honey and sunflowers. I sang until my voice cracked.

I asked Oshun to bless the child with life. And she did.

That little girl is now seven. She dances around the house and sings songs I used to sing to Oshun. She doesn't even know the words yet, but she knows the rhythm.

Oshun gave us a miracle. I will praise her for the rest of my days.

These stories remind us that Oshun isn't confined to ancient myths or distant rivers. She is alive in the hearts of her people. She flows through laughter, healing, music, dreams, and everyday acts of love.

Oshun doesn't ask for perfection, she asks for honesty. She responds to those who reach out with real emotion. Whether you are a lifelong devotee or just beginning to know her, these stories show that her energy is powerful, personal, and present.

She is the golden path that leads us back to ourselves.

14

OSHUN IN ART, FASHION, MUSIC, AND FILM

Oshun is more than a goddess worshipped in temples or honored at riversides. She is also a cultural force, alive in the rhythm of music, the glow of golden costumes, and the words of poets and filmmakers. Around the world, artists and performers call on her spirit to express beauty, joy, strength, and resistance.

From paintings and dance to music videos and literature, her image and energy have inspired generations of creators. Whether she is named directly or represented through symbols like water, honey, mirrors, or gold, Oshun shines brightly in the world of art and performance.

Oshun in Visual Art

Visual artists often turn to Oshun when they want to show the sacred feminine or the beauty of Black womanhood. In many paintings, she appears as a radiant figure dressed in yellow or gold. Her hair may be braided or flowing, and she is often surrounded by water, sunflowers, or peacocks, symbols linked to her identity.

Contemporary Paintings

Modern painters like Harmonia Rosales have reimagined classical art by replacing European figures with African deities, including Oshun. In Rosales' works, Oshun is shown as powerful and graceful, standing tall among the orishas or surrounded by symbols of life and abundance.

Other artists, such as Tamara Natalie Madden, have painted Oshun-inspired portraits that celebrate Black women as royal, magical, and divine. Madden's art is known for gold leaf accents and bright, bold colors, just like Oshun herself.

Photography and Digital Art

Oshun also lives in photography. Many photographers use gold lighting, flowing fabrics, and river settings to capture Oshun's essence in portraits. Digital artists often depict Oshun with glowing halos, golden eyes, and water pouring from her hands.

On platforms like Instagram and Pinterest, you'll find endless photo shoots where models dress in yellow and pose near water to honor Oshun. These images are more than fashion; they are acts of devotion and cultural pride.

Oshun in Dance and Costume

Dance is one of the oldest ways to honor the orishas. In Brazil, Cuba, and parts of the United States, dancers embody Oshun through movement, rhythm, and costume.

Afro-Brazilian Dance

In Candomblé ceremonies, Oshun, also known as Oxum, is honored with graceful, swaying movements. Dancers wear full, flowing skirts in bright yellow or golden fabric. The dance steps are gentle but powerful, like ripples on water. Each turn or wave of the hand reflects her presence as the goddess of rivers and love.

The dances often tell stories from Oshun's mythology, her search for love, her strength in sorrow, and her ability to heal with kindness. These performances take place in both sacred and public settings, blending worship with cultural celebration.

Carnaval Costumes

During Brazil's Carnaval, many samba schools create parades based on Yoruba deities. When Oxum is featured, you can expect an explosion of gold and glamour. Dancers wearing sparkling crowns, fans, and layered skirts move through the streets like living art. The music, movement, and costume together create a moment of joy that honors Oshun's beauty and influence.

Yemanjá and Oshun Fusion

Sometimes Oshun is celebrated alongside Yemanjá, another water orisha associated with the ocean. In dances and costumes, performers mix sea blue with Oshun's yellow and gold. This fusion reflects the connection between the two orishas and the wide reach of their symbolism in Afro-diasporic culture.

Oshun in Music

Music is one of the most powerful ways Oshun reaches new generations. Her presence in songs speaks to love, sweetness, confidence, and empowerment.

Traditional Songs

In Yorubaland and across the diaspora, traditional songs are sung to call on Oshun. These are often performed with drums, bells, and call-and-response vocals. The lyrics may describe her as "mother of the river," "sweet one," or "goddess of gold." Her songs are filled with praise and love, and they are used in rituals, festivals, and spiritual gatherings.

In Santería and Candomblé, these songs, called "oriki" or "cantigas", carry her stories and sacred names. The rhythm of the drums is said to call Oshun's energy down into the space, inviting her to dance and bless the people present.

Oshun in Contemporary Music

Today, many musicians reference Oshun in their work. She shows up in lyrics, album art, music videos, and even stage names.

One of the most well-known examples is Beyoncé, especially in her 2016 visual album *Lemonade*. In one powerful scene, Beyoncé wears a flowing yellow dress and walks through the streets, swinging a bat and breaking windows, smiling with fire and grace. This moment is widely seen as a tribute to Oshun, blending her sweet and fierce qualities. Water flows throughout the album, linking love, heartbreak, and healing, all themes tied to the Yoruba goddess Oshun.

There is also a music duo named OSHUN, comprising two women who create hip-hop and soul music inspired by African spirituality. Their lyrics often convey a sense of divine feminine energy, spiritual connection, and Black pride. They utilize their platform to educate about orishas and promote self-love and empowerment.

Rappers, reggae artists, and jazz musicians have all used Oshun as a symbol of beauty, power, and flow. Whether as metaphor or muse, Oshun's influence in music is as deep as the river she rules.

Oshun in Film and Literature

Writers and filmmakers have found ways to bring Oshun into books and movies. Her story has inspired characters, plots, and themes that transcend mythology and resonate with modern life.

Literature

In novels and poetry, Oshun often appears as a character or symbol of transformation. African American authors like Ntozake Shange, Toni Cade Bambara, and Lucille Clifton have written pieces that honor Oshun's strength and sweetness.

More recent books, especially in speculative and magical realism genres, feature Oshun-like figures who guide others through love, healing, or spiritual awakening. These stories remind us that orisha energy doesn't belong only in ancient times; it is alive in modern narratives, too.

Poets especially love writing about Oshun. Her softness and strength give writers rich images to explore. Honey, mirrors, rivers, gold, and laughter appear again and again as ways to express hope, joy, and beauty.

Film and Television

In films, Oshun's presence can be seen both directly and symbolically.

In *Daughters of the Dust* (1991), director Julie Dash weaves Yoruba traditions, including orisha stories, into a tale about African American women on the Sea Islands. The film is full of spiritual symbols, flowing dresses, and ocean scenes that nod to Oshun and other orishas.

In documentaries and spiritual series, Oshun is often introduced as a central figure in Yoruba religion and Black identity. She is depicted not just as a figure of the past, but as a living goddess whose presence continues to shape modern lives.

In short films and independent cinema, filmmakers from Nigeria, Brazil, Cuba, and the U.S. continue to include Oshun's energy in their work, sometimes through a mother character, a river spirit, or a fierce woman with a golden glow.

Oshun in Fashion and Style

Fashion is another powerful space where Oshun's influence shines. Designers, stylists, and everyday people use clothing and accessories to connect with her spirit.

Oshun-Inspired Fashion

Many fashion designers create clothing lines inspired by the Yoruba goddess Oshun. These outfits often include yellow and gold tones, flowing fabrics, floral prints, and shimmering textures. Designers use these styles to celebrate femininity, beauty, and the divine.

Runways in Nigeria, Brazil, and even New York have featured looks based on orisha traditions. The designs pay respect to spiritual roots while bringing Oshun's style into the modern world.

Everyday Style

People also honor Oshun through personal fashion. Wearing yellow on Fridays (her sacred day), gold jewelry, or flower crowns are all simple ways to show devotion. Some devotees paint their nails gold or carry small mirrors as a tribute.

Even makeup choices, such as gold highlighter, glowing skin, and bright lips, can reflect Oshun's radiant energy. It's not just about looks; it's about embodying joy, confidence, and sacred beauty.

Oshun and Black Feminism

Beyond art and beauty, Oshun has become a symbol of strength, self-worth, and resistance, especially in Black feminist movements.

Many Black women have reclaimed Oshun not just as a religious figure, but as a cultural symbol of healing and power. In a world that often tries to silence or ignore Black women, Oshun reminds them that softness is a form of strength, that joy is revolutionary, and that they are worthy of love and abundance.

Joy as Resistance

Black feminist writers and activists often speak of "joy as resistance." This means that expressing happiness, creativity, and pleasure is a way to resist and challenge systems of oppression. Oshun's energy fits perfectly into this idea. She teaches that beauty, love, and laughter are not just extras, they are part of survival and success.

In protest art, social media, and cultural events, Oshun's colors, symbols, and stories are used to inspire change and uplift voices. From poetry slams to visual campaigns, Oshun is a reminder of the sacred within every person, especially Black women and femmes.

Why Oshun Matters in Art

Oshun's presence in art matters for many reasons. She helps people:

- Connect with African roots and traditions
- Celebrate Black beauty and culture
- Feel empowered in their femininity or spiritual identity
- Find hope and healing through creativity

By showing up in paintings, songs, dances, and fashion, Oshun offers reminders of joy in a world that can feel heavy. She teaches that beauty and emotion are not weaknesses; they are sources of divine power.

Whether she is on a museum wall or a music stage, Oshun inspires people to be bold, kind, radiant, and free.

Oshun flows through the world of art like a golden river. She moves through the voices of singers, the hands of painters, and the feet of dancers. Her story is not trapped in the past. It is alive, in brushstrokes, lyrics, camera angles, and clothing.

In every form of expression, she reminds us of our own sacred worth. She shows us how to shine, how to soften, and how to stand strong.

As we've seen in this chapter, honoring Oshun through art is not just about beauty. It's about remembering who we are and how powerful love, joy, and spirit can be.

15

FESTIVALS, PUBLIC WORSHIP, AND SACRED SPACES

Worshipping Oshun is not just something that happens at a home altar or in quiet prayers. Around the world, people gather in joyful celebration to honor her in festivals, ceremonies, and public rituals. These gatherings are loud, beautiful, sacred, and filled with a sense of community energy. People come together to sing, dance, offer prayers, and express deep love for Oshun.

In this chapter, we will explore the powerful role of public worship in Oshun's tradition. We'll look at famous festivals like the Osun-Osogbo Festival in Nigeria, river pilgrimages in the diaspora, and how modern celebrations keep Oshun's spirit alive. We'll also learn how to take part in these sacred events with respect and care.

The Osun-Osogbo Festival: The Heart of Oshun Worship

The most famous and sacred celebration of Oshun is the Osun-Osogbo Festival, held every year in Osogbo, a city in south-western Nigeria. This two-week festival, held in August, attracts thousands of people from across Nigeria and around the world.

It is the most important public event dedicated to Oshun in Yoruba religion.

The Sacred Grove

The festival takes place at the Osun-Osogbo Sacred Grove, a lush forest by the Osun River. This grove is not just a beautiful park; it is a UNESCO World Heritage Site and considered one of the last sacred groves in Yoruba culture. It is believed to be Oshun's true spiritual home.

Inside the grove are shrines, sculptures, and sacred spaces dedicated to Oshun and other orishas. People walk barefoot on its paths, bring offerings, and pray for blessings. The river that flows through the grove is seen as Oshun herself, alive and listening.

Festival Origins

The Osun-Osogbo Festival has been celebrated for centuries. According to legend, the city of Osogbo was founded when early settlers discovered the Osun River. Oshun appeared to them and promised protection if they respected her sacred forest and held annual ceremonies in her honor. The people agreed, and the festival has been held ever since.

The festival serves as a means for the community to express gratitude to Oshun for fertility, health, peace, and prosperity. It is also a time to renew the spiritual bond between the people and the river goddess.

Rituals and Highlights

The festival begins with traditional rites performed by the Ataoja, the king of Osogbo, and the Osun priestesses. These include prayers, offerings, and sacred dances. Drums are played to invite the orishas, and chants fill the air.

The most important event is the procession to the river, led by the Arugba, a young virgin girl chosen to carry the sacred offering to Oshun. She wears white and walks with grace and silence, surrounded by priests, dancers, drummers, and devotees. The people follow her into the grove, singing and praying.

At the riverbank, the Arugba offers the sacrifices, usually food, honey, fruits, and other sacred items. Devotees bathe in the water, collect it in bottles, or pour it over their heads as a form of blessing. The river is believed to heal illness, bring fertility, and answer prayers.

The festival ends with more drumming, dancing, and joy. It is a time of healing, community, and celebration.

Other Festivals and Pilgrimages

While Osogbo hosts the most well-known Oshun festival, many other public events honoring her can be found across Africa and the diaspora. These include river pilgrimages, feast days, and local community celebrations.

River Pilgrimages in the Diaspora

In places like Cuba, Brazil, Trinidad, and Haiti, people honor Oshun, often referred to as Ochún or Oxum, by visiting rivers on special occasions. Devotees dress in yellow or white, sing sacred songs, and bring offerings such as honey, coins, oranges, and flowers.

In Cuba, during the Feast of Caridad del Cobre (the Catholic counterpart of Oshun), people walk or drive to rivers to pray for health, love, and abundance. In Brazil, during Festa de Iemanjá, many people also honor Oxum alongside the ocean goddess Iemanjá by offering flowers and candles to the water.

These river pilgrimages are deeply spiritual. The water is not just a symbol; it is a living connection to the divine. When people enter the river, they believe they are touching Oshun herself.

Community Celebrations

In cities with strong Afro-Caribbean or Afro-Brazilian populations, like Salvador, Havana, New Orleans, or Miami, Oshun is honored in parades, dance events, and spiritual services.

Some celebrations are open to the public, while others are held within spiritual houses or temples (called ile, terreiro, or casa depending on the tradition). These events may include drumming, ritual dances, storytelling, and food offerings.

Modern celebrations may also feature Oshun-inspired art shows, concerts, poetry readings, or wellness events focused on divine femininity and healing. In these spaces, Oshun continues to inspire creativity, unity, and joy.

How to Attend Public Worship Respectfully

Public festivals and river gatherings can be deeply moving experiences, even for those new to the Oshun tradition. But it's important to remember that these are not performances, they are sacred rituals. Here's how to show respect if you are attending or joining a public event for Oshun.

1. Learn Before You Go

Take time to understand what the event is about. Research Oshun, the orisha tradition, and the meaning behind the rituals. Ask organizers or spiritual leaders about the purpose of the event and how you should prepare.

If the event is part of a Santería or Candomblé service, it might be for initiated members only. In that case, don't attend unless invited. Always ask for permission first.

2. Dress with Respect

Wearing yellow or white is often encouraged, as these are the sacred colors of Oshun. Avoid wearing black (unless asked), and do not wear flashy or disrespectful clothing.

In many rituals, women wear skirts or dresses, and head coverings are common. Follow the dress code provided by event organizers or the spiritual community.

3. Follow the Flow

Watch and listen. If you're new, observe how others behave. Don't take pictures or record videos unless you're sure it's allowed. Many spiritual spaces forbid recording during rituals.

If people are singing or clapping, join in gently. If there's a moment of silence or prayer, be still. If you're asked to participate, such as placing flowers in the river or lighting a candle, do so with a respectful heart.

4. Bring an Offering (If Appropriate)

Some festivals invite visitors to bring offerings. For Oshun, these may include:

- Oranges or honey
- Yellow or white flowers
- Small coins (gold-colored if possible)
- Sweet treats like cakes or candies
- Perfume or scented oils

Always ask first, especially if you're visiting a sacred grove or river. Some places have rules about what can be left in nature to protect the environment.

5. Be Open, But Humble

You may experience a range of strong emotions, such as peace, joy, tears, or a sense of being connected to something bigger. That's beautiful. Let yourself experience the moment.

But remember that you are a guest in a spiritual home. Even if you feel a deep connection to Oshun, honor the elders, priests, and practitioners who have preserved these traditions for generations.

Contemporary Celebrations Around the World

Oshun's presence is expanding worldwide. As more people explore African spirituality, they create new ways to celebrate her that mix tradition with modern life.

New Moon Circles

In some spiritual communities, especially in the U.S. and Europe, people gather in small groups to honor Oshun during the new moon. These events often include:

- Guided meditations
- Journaling or affirmations
- Sharing honey and fruit
- Setting intentions for love, healing, or abundance

While not part of traditional Yoruba religion, these new practices are inspired by Oshun's energy, allowing people to connect with her in a personal and creative way.

Women's Retreats and Healing Spaces

Oshun is also honored in retreats and workshops focused on divine femininity, emotional healing, and creative expression.

These events may use storytelling, dance, yoga, and art to connect with Oshun's themes of joy, beauty, and balance.

Some retreats include river visits, sacred baths, or altar building. These gatherings bring together people of all backgrounds who feel called to Oshun's energy.

Online Ceremonies

With the growth of the internet, many people now attend virtual Oshun events. These can include:

- Live-streamed river blessings
- Zoom rituals and full moon gatherings
- Online prayer circles or Oshun-themed meditations
- Social media campaigns using the hashtag #Oshun or #OshunBlessings

These digital spaces allow those who may not have a local community to still connect with Oshun in meaningful ways.

Sacred Spaces Beyond the Grove

While the Osun-Osogbo Grove is the most famous sacred site for Oshun, many people have created other powerful spaces to honor her around the world.

Shrines and Altars

Many temples, homes, and community spaces have dedicated altars to Oshun. These may include:

- A bowl of fresh water or river water
- Mirrors, gold coins, or peacock feathers
- Yellow candles or flowers
- Statues or pictures of Oshun

People visit these altars to pray, offer thanks, or ask for help with love, health, or abundance. These spaces become personal rivers of connection to Oshun's energy.

Oshun Gardens and Parks

Some cities have parks or gardens inspired by the Yoruba goddess Oshun. These places include flowing water, golden flowers, and sculptures that reflect her presence. They serve as peaceful spots for meditation, prayer, or community events.

In Miami, for example, some cultural centers host Oshun-themed art exhibits or offer spiritual classes related to orisha traditions. These public events keep the river of worship flowing through art and education.

The Joy of Collective Devotion

Worshipping Oshun in a group, whether at a festival, by a river, or in a dance circle, is a powerful experience. These gatherings remind us that faith is not just personal; it is also a shared experience. Public worship fosters community, connects generations, and preserves sacred traditions.

The Osun-Osogbo Festival, river pilgrimages, and diasporic ceremonies are not just events; they are also expressions of a rich cultural heritage. They are expressions of love, gratitude, and connection to something divine. They invite everyone, elders, children, locals, and travelers, to dance with joy, honor with humility, and celebrate life with an open heart.

When we gather to honor Oshun, we create sacred space not just on land, but in our hearts. Together, we become rivers of devotion, flowing with grace, beauty, and love.

16

OSHUN'S ETHICAL TEACHINGS

MANY PEOPLE KNOW OSHUN AS A GODDESS OF BEAUTY, LOVE, AND the sweet river. But underneath her golden shine lies something deeper, a strong moral center. Oshun is more than charming. She is wise, fair, and deeply rooted in values that guide not just how we feel, but how we live.

In the Yoruba spiritual tradition, Oshun is known for her sense of justice, truth, and balance. She not only gives blessings to those who pray for love or abundance, but also to those who pray for healing or protection. She also teaches people how to treat others, how to carry themselves with dignity, and how to walk through the world with both grace and strength.

In this chapter, we will explore Oshun's ethical teachings, what they are, why they matter, and how to practice them in everyday life. Her lessons are powerful tools for building better relationships, fairer communities, and more loving lives.

Kindness and Compassion: Oshun's Heart

One of Oshun's most important teachings is the power of kindness. She reminds us that caring for others is not just a nice thing to do, it is a spiritual duty. In many stories, Oshun assists those who are in need. She listens, she gives, and she comforts.

Giving from the Heart

Oshun is a giver. In her stories, she offers honey, food, healing water, and even her own time and energy to help those in need. She doesn't give because she has to; she gives because it is part of her nature. For Oshun, generosity is an act of love and a form of leadership.

Kindness is not about being weak or trying to please everyone. Instead, Oshun teaches that real strength comes from being gentle even when it's hard. She shows that soft words can calm anger, just as her river cools the sun's fire.

Compassion Without Judgment

Another key value Oshun teaches is compassion without judgment. In several myths, Oshun helps those who feel ashamed or broken. She never laughs at their pain. She listens. She brings comfort and encouragement.

This kind of compassion asks us to see the whole person, not just their mistakes or their struggles. Oshun wants us to treat others with dignity, even if we don't agree with them. In her eyes, everyone deserves love, support, and a chance to grow.

Sweetness and Strength: A Delicate Balance

Oshun is often called the "sweet one," but she is not always sweet. She knows when to smile, and when to speak firmly. She teaches that knowing when to be gentle and when to be firm is a key aspect of spiritual wisdom.

The Power of Softness

There is great power in softness. Oshun shows that charm, kindness, and joy can change hearts and open doors. In one myth, when the other orishas could not make the world work, they ignored Oshun. But the world stayed broken until she stepped in with her grace and wisdom. She didn't use force, she used love, and it worked.

Sweetness can bring healing, end arguments, and create peace. But it must come from a place of self-respect. Oshun is not sweet because she needs approval; she is sweet because she chooses to be.

Setting Boundaries

But sweetness doesn't mean letting people walk all over you. Oshun also teaches us how to say "no" when needed. In several stories, she sets clear boundaries. If someone disrespects her, she does not just smile and move on. She stands up for herself. Sometimes she even withdraws her blessings to teach a lesson.

In life, this means knowing when to speak up, when to protect your energy, and when to step back. Oshun reminds us that being spiritual does not mean being passive. You can be kind and still have strong boundaries.

Myths That Teach Ethical Lessons

Oshun's stories are full of wisdom. Through them, she teaches about honesty, humility, and emotional intelligence. Let's look at a few myths that reveal her moral teachings.

The Myth of Oshun Saving the World

In one famous myth, the orishas were sent to Earth to create the world. But they ignored Oshun because she was a woman. They tried to shape the world with power and control, but everything they built fell apart. Crops would not grow. Rivers dried up. People were unhappy.

Oshun stayed quiet at first. But when things got bad enough, she stepped forward. She sang, danced, and brought offerings to Olodumare, the Supreme Creator. Her sweetness and devotion moved the divine heart. The world was healed, and balance returned.

Lesson: Never underestimate the power of softness. Just because something looks gentle doesn't mean it's not strong. Respect every voice at the table, including the quiet ones.

The Myth of Oshun and the Dry River

In another story, Oshun became angry after being disrespected by the other orishas. She left, taking her river with her. The land dried up. The people became thirsty and sick. The other orishas begged her to return. Only after they apologized and honored her properly did she bring her river back.

Lesson: If people ignore your worth, it's okay to remove your energy. You do not have to give to those who do not appreciate you. Your time, love, and presence are sacred.

The Story of the Woman and the Honey

A woman once came to Oshun for help with a difficult relationship. Oshun told her to stop speaking harshly and start using honey in her words. The woman followed the advice. She became calmer, more thoughtful, and more open. The relationship improved, not because she forced it, but because she changed the way she communicated.

Lesson: Words matter. Tone matters. Even in hard conversations, sweetness can be more powerful than anger.

Humility: The Grace to Stay Grounded

Another value Oshun teaches is humility. Even though she is beautiful, powerful, and beloved, she does not act as if she is better than others. She knows her worth, but she doesn't use it to make others feel small.

Confidence vs. Pride

There's a difference between being confident and being prideful. Oshun wants us to know we are beautiful, strong, and worthy, but also to remember that we are still learning. Being humble means being open to growth, listening to others, and not needing to prove anything.

In many stories, Oshun is willing to serve others, work with them, or even step back when needed. She doesn't always have to be in charge. She leads with grace, not ego.

Honoring the Whole Community

Oshun reminds us that no one rises alone. When she gives blessings, she does it to uplift the whole community. In public festivals and river rituals, the joy is shared. The offerings are shared. The healing is shared.

This teaches us that ethical living is not just about personal gain; it is also about the greater good. It's about doing what's good for the whole, not just the self.

Applying Oshun's Ethics to Modern Life

Now that we've explored Oshun's values, let's look at how to apply them in everyday life, at home, in relationships, at work, and in the world.

In Love and Friendship

- Be generous with your kindness, but also honest about your needs
- Use sweet words to express love, even when you're upset
- Know your worth. If someone does not respect it, step back like Oshun did
- Celebrate beauty, joy, and affection, it's part of spiritual connection

In Work and Leadership

- Lead with grace, not fear
- Support others and lift them up, success is sweeter when shared
- Speak with care. A kind voice can open more doors than a loud one
- Know when to step in and when to listen, balance is key

In Daily Choices

- Choose compassion before judgment
- Stay soft without being weak
- Stand firm when your values are tested
- Share your blessings. Oshun flows where generosity flows

Creating Ethical Rituals Inspired by Oshun

You can also develop spiritual practices centered on Oshun's moral lessons. Here are a few simple ideas:

1. Sweet Speech Reflection

Each morning, place a small bowl of honey on your altar or kitchen counter. Before speaking to anyone, touch the honey and remind yourself to speak kindly that day. Ask Oshun to guide your words with sweetness and honesty.

2. Boundary Candle Ritual

Light a yellow candle and write down something you need to say "no" to. Say a prayer to Oshun asking for clarity and courage. Burn the note (safely) and let the candle remind you that protecting your energy is a sacred act.

3. Gratitude Sharing Practice

Each week, give something of value to someone else, a meal, a note, a helping hand. Say a prayer to Oshun asking that your giving ripple out into the world. Remind yourself that generosity creates spiritual flow.

Living the Golden Path

Oshun is a goddess of rivers, beauty, and love. But she is also a teacher of ethics, emotional intelligence, and sacred strength. She invites us to live with kindness, but not to be naive. She encourages sweetness, but also boundaries. She inspires humility, but not self-erasure.

To walk Oshun's path is to live in balance, to give and receive, to speak with care, and to lead with heart. Her ethical teachings are not just ancient wisdom; they are practical guides for modern life.

In a world that often praises power without love, Oshun offers a different model: one where sweetness is strong, where leadership is graceful, and where love is both a gift and a responsibility.

May we learn from her. May we live like her. And may we never forget that true beauty shines brightest when it flows from a heart that honors both itself and others.

17
EVERYDAY APPLICATIONS OF OSHUN'S WISDOM

To live in flow is to move through life like a river, strong, graceful, and always in motion. It means trusting your feelings, staying open to joy, and knowing when to move forward or rest. Oshun, as the goddess of rivers and sweet water, teaches us how to live this way.

Flow isn't just about going with the wind. It's about living in balance. It's about listening to your heart and using both your strength and softness to guide your choices. Living in flow means you don't have to force things. You let life unfold while keeping your values close at hand.

Whether it's in how you speak to yourself, handle relationships, approach work, or create your home environment, Oshun's wisdom can guide you to live with more love, joy, and ease.

Flow in Relationships

Relationships are one of the most important parts of our lives. They can bring joy, comfort, and growth. Oshun is the orisha of love, sweetness, and connection. She teaches us how to build healthy, beautiful bonds with others and with ourselves.

Speaking with Care

Oshun teaches that words are powerful. They can heal or harm, depending on how they're used. In your relationships, take time to speak with love, especially during disagreements. Instead of shouting or blaming, try pausing and expressing your feelings calmly.

For example, instead of saying, *"You never listen to me,"* try, *"I feel hurt when I don't feel heard."* That small shift can open the door to understanding instead of conflict.

Listening with an Open Heart

Oshun reminds us that listening is just as important as speaking. Practice really hearing others, not just waiting for your turn to talk. This helps build trust and shows that you value their thoughts and feelings.

In romantic relationships, friendships, and family life, being a kind listener brings you closer to the people you care about.

Knowing When to Let Go

Just as rivers flow around rocks, sometimes we need to let go of relationships that block our peace. Oshun teaches us to love ourselves enough to move on from what no longer serves us. This is not cruel, it's healing.

Ending a friendship or relationship doesn't mean you failed. It means you are making room for something better and more aligned with your spirit.

Self-Talk and Inner Flow

How you talk to yourself shapes your entire life. Oshun teaches us that loving yourself is a sacred act. She carries mirrors not for vanity, but for self-reflection and truth. When we learn to speak kindly to ourselves, everything starts to change.

Mirror Talk Practice

Each morning, look at yourself in the mirror. Speak to yourself like you would speak to a loved one. Say things like:

- *"You are enough."*
- *"You are growing, and that's beautiful."*
- *"You deserve love and rest."*

Doing this daily helps you build inner strength and teaches your mind to trust your heart.

Being Gentle with Mistakes

Everyone makes mistakes. Oshun's energy reminds us not to punish ourselves for being human. When you make a mistake, take responsibility, but also show yourself compassion. Ask, *"What can I learn?"* instead of saying, *"I'm not good enough."*

Self-forgiveness is part of emotional flow. Holding on to guilt stops the water. Let it go so your spirit can move again.

Flow in Career and Purpose

Your career or schoolwork can also be a part of your spiritual journey. Oshun supports abundance, creativity, and success, but only when those things come from alignment, not stress or fear.

Aligning with Purpose

Ask yourself, *"Does what I do bring joy to me or to others?"* If you feel empty, stuck, or bored, it may be time to adjust your path. That doesn't mean quitting everything. It could mean:

- Adding creative projects to your day
- Asking for new tasks at work
- Exploring what lights you up outside your job

Oshun wants you to create, express, and shine. She supports people who lead with love and serve with joy.

Letting Go of the Hustle Mentality

Oshun is abundant, but she is not rushed. Her blessings flow through ease, not burnout. In your work life, remember that rest is a productive activity. You don't have to earn your worth through overwork.

Take breaks. Take walks. Laugh during your lunch. The more you take care of your spirit, the better your work will be.

Making Decisions in Flow

One of the most powerful lessons Oshun offers is trusting your inner voice. When faced with big or small decisions, you can learn to choose with both heart and wisdom.

The Yes and No Exercise

When you're unsure about something, ask your body:

- Does saying yes feel light or heavy?
- Does saying no feel calm or anxious?

This helps you practice what many call intuition, a feeling-based inner compass. Oshun encourages you to trust it.

Sometimes you may not know the full path ahead. That's okay. Take the next best step and let the rest unfold. Water doesn't need to see the whole river to keep moving.

Following Joy

If you're stuck between choices, ask yourself: *"Which one brings me closer to joy?"* Joy is not selfish. It's a sign that you're walking your true path.

Oshun's flow moves toward what feels nourishing, not what drains you. Choose the life that makes you feel alive.

Flow in Rest and Rhythm

Oshun is deeply connected to the natural rhythms of life, tides, seasons, and cycles. She shows us that rest is sacred and that slowness can be a beautiful thing.

Creating a Rest Practice

Just as we set aside time for work and chores, we should also set aside time for rest. This can be:

- A weekly "sweet hour" where you do something purely enjoyable
- Turning off your phone to sit by a window or go outside
- Soaking your feet in warm water while listening to soft music

This is not laziness, it's soul care. You are not a machine. You are a spirit in a body. You deserve to slow down and take a breath.

Honor the Moon and the Water

Oshun is connected to the moon, tides, and water. Create rituals that match these rhythms:

- **New moon**: Set intentions for joy and love
- **Full moon**: Release stress and fears in a bath or river

- **Daily water moments**: Whisper a blessing when you drink water or wash your face

These small acts help you stay connected to Oshun's gentle flow.

A Lifestyle of Beauty and Gratitude

Oshun teaches that life is meant to be **beautiful**. Not perfect, beautiful in spirit, heart, and intention. You can live in beauty, regardless of your situation.

Surrounding Yourself with Light

You don't need gold jewelry or expensive things to honor beauty. Simple changes can create a more Oshun-like space:

- Place fresh flowers in your room
- Light candles with a joyful heart
- Play music that makes you feel soft and powerful
- Keep a small bowl of oranges or sweets as a sign of sweetness

Let your home reflect your inner world. Let it remind you that you are loved.

Gratitude as a River

Each night, write down three things you're thankful for. They don't have to be big:

- *"I had a peaceful walk."*
- *"My friend made me laugh."*
- *"I cooked something delicious."*

Gratitude opens the river of flow. When we focus on what's working, more begins to work.

Flow with Others and the World

Living in flow also means knowing your part in the bigger picture. Oshun wants us to **care for others, honor nature, and build joyful communities**.

Random Acts of Sweetness

Give out love freely, without expecting anything back. Some ideas:

- Compliment someone sincerely
- Help someone carry something
- Leave a kind note for a friend or a stranger

Oshun's energy spreads when kindness moves through us.

Flowing with Nature

Take time to be near rivers, lakes, or any natural water source. Listen. Offer a flower. Say thank you. Let nature remind you that everything moves, and you are part of that sacred flow.

Living the Flow Every Day

Here's a simple guide you can return to as you practice living in Oshun's flow.

Area How to Flow with Oshun

Area	How to Flow with Oshun
Relationships	Speak kindly, listen well, and release what blocks your peace.
Self-Talk	Use gentle, loving words to build your confidence.
Work/School	Lead with joy, rest often, and create with heart.
Decisions	Trust your gut. Choose what feels light, true, and joyful.
Rest	Make space for calm, beauty, and emotional stillness.
Gratitude	Notice life's small gifts and say thank you often.
Community	Be generous, helpful, and joyful with others.

Let the River Guide You

Oshun is always flowing. She is always speaking through water, dreams, beauty, and love. Living in her flow doesn't mean everything is easy. It means you move with grace, even when things are hard. You don't rush, but you don't stay stuck. You let life shape you like the river shapes the land.

As you move forward, carry these truths with you:

- You are allowed to rest.
- You are allowed to shine.
- You are allowed to say no.

- You are allowed to feel deeply.
- You are allowed to grow.

Oshun walks beside you in every step of joy, every sip of water, every word of sweetness. Let her spirit remind you that life is not a race. It is a river. Let it flow.

ALIGNING WITH OSHUN'S ENERGY

THIS 30-DAY JOURNEY IS DESIGNED TO HELP YOU CONNECT WITH Oshun's energy daily. Each day offers a short theme, a guiding affirmation, a reflection question, and a micro-ritual. These small steps add up to real change in your heart, mind, spirit, and life.

You don't need any special tools to begin. Just your attention, your heart, and your willingness to show up each day.

Whether you choose to do this practice in the morning, before bed, or during a quiet moment in your day, let it be a sacred time just for you.

Daily Practice Format

For each of the 30 days, you'll find:

- **Theme** – A word or idea inspired by Oshun
- **Affirmation** – A sentence to repeat and believe
- **Reflection** – A journal or meditation prompt
- **Micro-Ritual** – A 5-minute spiritual or self-care action

You can use a notebook to write your thoughts or just pause and reflect.

Week 1: Opening to Love

Day 1 – Sweetness

Affirmation: "*I welcome sweetness into my life.*"

Reflection: What does sweetness feel like in my body, my mood, or my words?

Micro-Ritual: Add a teaspoon of honey to your tea or eat a piece of fruit mindfully. As you enjoy it, give thanks to Oshun.

Day 2 – Flow

Affirmation: "*I let life flow through me.*"

Reflection: Where in my life am I trying to force things? What would it feel like to let go?

Micro-Ritual: Pour a glass of water. Hold it and ask Oshun to help you release control. Drink slowly.

Day 3 – Love

Affirmation: "I am worthy of love just as I am."

Reflection: How do I show myself love today?

Micro-Ritual: Light a candle and say your affirmation out loud. Gaze into a mirror and smile gently.

Day 4 – Self-Acceptance

Affirmation: "I accept all parts of myself with compassion."

Reflection: What parts of me have I judged or hidden? Can I offer them kindness today?

Micro-Ritual: Write a short love letter to yourself.

Day 5 – Connection

Affirmation: "My heart is open to meaningful connections."

Reflection: Who makes me feel safe and loved?

Micro-Ritual: Send a kind message to someone you care about.

Day 6 – Sensuality

Affirmation: "My senses are sacred."

Reflection: How can I enjoy my body without judgment today?

Micro-Ritual: Apply lotion, oil, or perfume with care and attention. Thank your body.

Day 7 – Trust

Affirmation: "I trust my emotions to guide me."

Reflection: What is one feeling I've been avoiding? What is it teaching me?

Micro-Ritual: Sit quietly near water or listen to flowing sounds. Breathe deeply and listen to your heart.

Week 2: Awakening Joy

Day 8 – Play

Affirmation: "I give myself permission to play."

Reflection: What activity brings me joy for no reason?

Micro-Ritual: Do something just for fun, draw, dance, sing, or skip.

Day 9 – Music

Affirmation: "I move in rhythm with life."

Reflection: What kind of music lifts my spirit?

Micro-Ritual: Play a song that makes you smile. Move your body freely.

Day 10 – Gratitude

Affirmation: "Gratitude opens my heart."

Reflection: What three things can I be thankful for right now?

Micro-Ritual: Write a gratitude list on a piece of paper and place it on your altar or dresser.

Day 11 – Laughter

Affirmation: "Laughter heals me."

Reflection: What made me laugh recently?

Micro-Ritual: Watch or read something funny. Let your laughter be medicine.

Day 12 – Beauty

Affirmation: "I see beauty all around me."

Reflection: What do I find beautiful in myself today?

Micro-Ritual: Place a flower or something lovely where you'll see it often today.

Day 13 – Receiving

Affirmation: "I allow myself to receive love, help, and joy."

Reflection: When was the last time I let someone support me?

Micro-Ritual: Ask for help today, even in a small way.

Day 14 – Celebration

Affirmation: "Every part of me deserves celebration."

Reflection: What am I proud of right now?

Micro-Ritual: Make a toast to yourself with water or juice. Say "To my joy!"

Week 3: Embracing Abundance

Day 15 – Abundance

Affirmation: "I live in a world of abundance."

Reflection: What does abundance look like for me beyond money?

Micro-Ritual: Place 5 coins or bills in a bowl. Whisper your financial wishes and express your gratitude.

Day 16 – Worth

Affirmation: "I am worthy of every good thing."

Reflection: What old beliefs have made me feel unworthy?

Micro-Ritual: Write down one unhelpful belief. Burn or tear it up. Speak your affirmation aloud.

Day 17 – Flow of Money

Affirmation: "Money flows to me with ease."

Reflection: How do I feel when I receive money?

Micro-Ritual: Clean your wallet or purse and sprinkle a drop of cinnamon inside as a blessing.

Day 18 – Generosity

Affirmation: "I give with joy and an open heart."

Reflection: What can I give today, time, love, kindness, or something else?

Micro-Ritual: Give someone a small gift or a surprise note.

Day 19 – Purpose

Affirmation: "I follow the path that brings me alive."

Reflection: What activity or topic makes me feel most alive?

Micro-Ritual: Spend 15 minutes today doing or exploring that thing.

Day 20 – Alignment

Affirmation: "I align my life with love and joy."

Reflection: What aspects of my daily routine feel forced or burdensome?

Micro-Ritual: Choose one small task to do more mindfully today.

Day 21 – Overflow

Affirmation: "My joy overflows into the world."

Reflection: Who in my life could use encouragement today?

Micro-Ritual: Write a sweet note, text, or message and send it with love.

Week 4: Living with Intuition and Grace

Day 22 – Intuition

Affirmation: "My intuition is wise and clear."

Reflection: When was the last time I trusted my gut, and did it work out?

Micro-Ritual: Ask your inner voice a yes/no question. Listen quietly.

Day 23 – Calm

Affirmation: "I choose calm over chaos."

Reflection: What helps me feel peaceful, even during stress?

Micro-Ritual: Light a candle and sit quietly for 5 minutes. Breathe slowly.

Day 24 – Boundaries

Affirmation: "I honor myself by setting kind boundaries."

Reflection: Where in my life do I need clearer boundaries?

Micro-Ritual: Say "no" to one thing today that doesn't feel good.

Day 25 – Reflection

Affirmation: "I learn and grow from every experience."

Reflection: What has Oshun shown me so far in this journey?

Micro-Ritual: Write a journal entry titled "What I Know Now."

Day 26 – Clarity

Affirmation: "I see clearly and choose wisely."

Reflection: Is there a decision I've been avoiding?

Micro-Ritual: Write down your options. Sit with them in silence, then underline the one that feels most true to you.

Day 27 – Renewal

Affirmation: "Every day is a new beginning."

Reflection: What would I do if I were to give myself a fresh start?

Micro-Ritual: Take a warm bath or shower and imagine old energy washing away.

Day 28 – Softness

Affirmation: "My softness is a strength."

Reflection: When have I hidden my soft side?

Micro-Ritual: Wrap yourself in a blanket and listen to gentle music. Allow your body to fully relax.

Closing Days: Integration and Blessing

Day 29 – Blessing

Affirmation: "I am blessed and blessing others."

Reflection: How have I changed over the past month?

Micro-Ritual: Write yourself a blessing or prayer. Speak it out loud.

Day 30 – Devotion

Affirmation: "I walk in devotion to beauty, love, and joy."

Reflection: How can I continue this connection with Oshun beyond today?

Micro-Ritual: Place a small bowl of water, honey, or flowers on your altar. Whisper your gratitude.

Final Journal Questions

Take time after the 30 days to reflect:

- What did I learn about myself?
- What surprised me?
- What was the hardest day, and why?
- What was the sweetest moment of flow?
- How do I feel now compared to when I started?

Living in Flow Beyond 30 Days

You don't have to stop at Day 30. This practice can grow and change with you. You can:

- Repeat the 30 days with new reflections
- Focus on one theme each week
- Share the practice with friends or a spiritual group
- Add new micro-rituals that fit your daily life

Most importantly, remember: you are the river. You are not stuck. You are not broken. You are flowing, changing, and becoming more of your true self every day.

Let Oshun's energy live in you, through joy, kindness, beauty, and peace.

19

OSHUN'S SPIRIT IN TODAY'S WORLD

IN TODAY'S CHANGING WORLD, MANY PEOPLE ARE TURNING TO OLD wisdom to find new answers. One of the most powerful guides for this time is Oshun, the orisha of love, rivers, beauty, and divine femininity. Her spirit is more than just ancient mythology; it is a living energy that resonates with people today who are working towards healing, justice, and a better future.

Oshun is more than a symbol of beauty and joy. She is also a force of change, a protector of nature, and a guide for those who believe in compassion, balance, and respect for life. In this chapter, we examine how Oshun's energy is resurging, not only in personal devotion but also in global movements for justice, healing, and spiritual awakening.

Oshun and Environmental Justice

One of the most significant ways Oshun manifests today is through the fight for clean water and environmental protection. As the orisha of rivers and freshwater, she is deeply connected to the Earth's health. In many African and Afro-diasporic communities, Oshun is seen as a guardian of water. Without clean rivers and safe water, life cannot thrive, and Oshun cannot fully flow.

Across the world, water is in danger. Pollution, climate change, and unfair systems often take away clean water from poor and marginalized communities. In many places, Indigenous people and people of African descent are the most affected. This is why Oshun has become a spiritual symbol in water justice movements.

Activists and spiritual leaders who follow Oshun often join forces to protect rivers, halt pipelines, and combat pollution. In Nigeria, for example, the Osun River, named after the orisha herself, is sacred. People pray and give offerings at the river. But pollution and development have put it at risk. Some Oshun devotees now work to clean and protect it, understanding that caring for the river is a way to care for Oshun.

In the Americas, too, Oshun's presence has been felt in the realm of water justice. At protests for clean water, like those in Flint, Michigan, or Standing Rock, some people have called on Oshun through prayers, songs, and ceremonies. They understand that Oshun's love is not passive, it's powerful. It brings life, but it also fights for it.

Feminine Power as Resistance

Oshun is a goddess, but she is also a mirror for feminine power in all its forms. Some people misunderstand her as only sweet, soft, or pretty. But Oshun's power goes much deeper. She teaches that being feminine does not mean being weak. In fact, her beauty and softness are part of her strength. She is a warrior of emotion, a speaker of truth, and a master of balance.

In modern feminism, especially Black feminism and Afro-feminism, Oshun has become an important symbol. Many women and femmes look to her as a model for healing from harm, reclaiming power, and loving themselves fully. Through Oshun, they learn that being emotional is not a flaw, it's a gift. Feeling deeply, loving freely, and protecting what you care about is sacred work.

Some writers, artists, and speakers refer to "Oshun energy" as the ability to lead with love while remaining grounded. This energy helps people set boundaries, speak up against injustice, and still find beauty in their lives. For those who face racism, sexism, or violence, Oshun becomes a guide who says, *"You are worthy. You are powerful. You are divine."*

Decolonizing Spirituality

For hundreds of years, African religions were pushed underground. Colonizers told people that their gods were evil and forced them to follow new religions. But today, many are reclaiming their ancestral paths. In this process, Oshun is often one of the first orishas people meet.

Reclaiming Oshun is an act of decolonization. It's a way of saying: *"My roots matter. My ancestors matter. My culture is sacred."* People across the Americas, from Brazil to Cuba to the United States, are learning the names and stories of the orishas that were once hidden.

Many young people of African descent are turning back to Oshun not only for spiritual reasons but to heal the wounds of racism, displacement, and cultural loss. By honoring Oshun, they reconnect with something that was never truly lost, only waiting to be remembered.

This is not always easy. It takes learning, listening, and often working with elders. But Oshun teaches patience. She invites people to the river, not with force, but with sweetness. She says, *"Come. Remember who you are."*

Oshun in Modern Activism and Healing Spaces

Oshun's energy is flowing in the hearts of those fighting for justice, healing, and peace. Her presence is not limited to rivers or shrines; it is also evident in community gatherings, healing circles, protests, and even classrooms. When people come together to speak truth, care for one another, and work toward change, Oshun is there.

In many healing spaces led by Black women, queer individuals, and spiritual teachers, Oshun is invoked as a sacred guide. Her presence brings gentleness and safety, helping people feel seen and supported. She teaches that healing doesn't always happen alone, it can bloom in groups, in movement, in music, and in shared love.

For example, some therapists and community healers incorporate Oshun's symbols, such as honey, mirrors, or water, into their work. A yellow cloth on a table, a bowl of fresh water, or a soft candle flame can bring her warmth into a room. These simple touches help people remember: healing is beautiful. It doesn't have to be rushed or forced. It can unfold gently, like the flow of a river.

In activism, Oshun's power helps balance rage with care. Anger is a natural response when people are hurt or oppressed. However, Oshun teaches that anger must be guided by love and a higher purpose. She doesn't tell us to forget injustice; she teaches us how to respond with grace, cleverness, and courage.

Some protest organizers invoke Oshun to bring emotional balance into the struggle. They use her energy to keep hope alive, even when the work is hard. Her power reminds people to rest, to cry, to dance, and to keep going. In these ways, Oshun becomes not just a goddess, but a way of being in the world.

Oshun and the Creative Spirit

Art has always been one of Oshun's favorite tools. Her love for beauty, color, and movement inspires artists of all kinds. From painting and poetry to dance and film, her energy brings passion and imagination to life.

Today, many renowned artists pay homage to Oshun through their work. But Oshun's influence goes beyond celebrities. In cities across the world, murals of Oshun shine on walls. Community dancers perform in yellow and gold. Writers and poets speak her name as they share stories of love, healing, and rebirth. Her colors, her stories, and her strength continue to inspire.

In Brazil, during the Festa de Iemanjá (which also honors water goddesses); people wear white and offer flowers and gifts to the sea. Although Iemanjá is often regarded as a distinct orisha, the celebrations frequently include praise for Oxum (Oshun), her freshwater counterpart. These festivals remind people that honoring Oshun is not just about the past, it is about creating joy and beauty in the present.

Community Care as Sacred Work

In Oshun's teachings, care for the community is sacred. She reminds us that love is not just romantic, it is a responsibility. She teaches us to look after our neighbors, to feed the hungry, to care for children, and to bring light into dark times.

In many communities, particularly those rooted in Afro-diasporic traditions, Oshun is the heart of spiritual and emotional care. Her shrines may be places of beauty, but they are also places where people find hope. Her prayers are not only for personal gain, but also for the healing of families, the care of the sick, and the easing of grief.

Oshun shows us that nurturing others is powerful. Cooking for someone, offering a hug, or simply sitting in silence with someone in pain, these are all acts of divine service. They do not need to be big or loud to matter.

Today, many grassroots organizations that support women's health, mental wellness, or spiritual growth draw strength from Oshun. Whether through therapy, food programs, or art therapy circles, her gentle influence encourages acts of radical compassion, especially for those who are often ignored or forgotten.

Rest, Pleasure, and Joy as Resistance

In a world that often pushes people to work endlessly and forget their worth, Oshun whispers something different. She says, 'You are already enough.' You deserve to feel good. You are allowed to rest.

Rest is not laziness; it is a form of healing. Taking time to breathe, to laugh, to eat well, to sleep deeply, and to enjoy life is an act of resistance in a system that values production over people. Oshun teaches that pleasure is sacred. Dancing, soaking in a warm bath, enjoying sweet fruit, or dressing in bright colors are all ways to honor her, and yourself.

For those facing injustice, joy can seem elusive. But Oshun reminds us that joy is a birthright, not a reward. By creating moments of joy, people reclaim their humanity. In Oshun's eyes, smiling in hard times is not denial, it is strength.

Movements like The Nap Ministry, Pleasure Activism, and others all echo Oshun's wisdom. They say: rest is medicine, softness is power, and caring for yourself is a radical act. These ideas come from the same spirit that Oshun brings into the world.

The Future of Oshun's Worship

Oshun's worship has survived for centuries, even through forced migration, slavery, colonization, and oppression. Today, her spirit continues to grow, touching the hearts of people all over the world, both those rooted in Yoruba culture and those newly discovering her. Her presence is expanding into spiritual circles, healing communities, and modern wellness and justice practices.

In the past, Oshun's ceremonies were held by elders and spiritual leaders trained in Ifá or Santería. While that is still very important, today, many people also honor Oshun in their own way, through meditation, prayer, dance, poetry, or by placing flowers and honey by a river. This kind of devotion may take different forms, but it still reflects love, respect, and a desire to connect.

People of all backgrounds are learning how to honor African deities in ways that are respectful and non-appropriative. Many are reading books, studying history, attending ceremonies (with permission), and listening to elders from Yoruba or Afro-Caribbean traditions. This kind of care helps ensure that Oshun's worship is honored, not just copied.

At the same time, younger generations are feeling empowered to reclaim spiritual practices that were once hidden or shamed. Many Black, Latinx, and Indigenous youth are returning to ancestral faiths, and Oshun is often one of the first to call them home. Through her, they find a source of strength, love, and pride.

Social media has also played a part in sharing Oshun's image and energy. While this brings attention and interest, it also brings responsibility. Her sacred traditions are not just "aesthetic" or trends; they are living, breathing practices rooted in community, respect, and deep wisdom. As Oshun becomes more visible, a growing movement emerges to preserve the depth of her path.

Oshun in a Changing World

We live in a time of major change, climate shifts, social unrest, economic struggles, and personal challenges are happening all over the globe. In the middle of this, Oshun's teachings are more important than ever.

She teaches us to care for the Earth. Her rivers remind us that water is life, and that without it, nothing can grow. She calls us to fight for clean water for all people, especially in places where access is limited due to pollution, poverty, or injustice. Her presence is evident in environmental movements, particularly those led by women, people of color, and Indigenous communities.

Oshun also reminds us to care for each other. As people struggle with loneliness, mental health challenges, and disconnection, her energy becomes a bridge to healing. Her way is not harsh or judgmental; it is soft, loving, and full of acceptance. She teaches us how to forgive, how to trust, and how to build strong, loving relationships with others and with ourselves.

In a world that often values power over kindness, Oshun teaches that true power comes from love, not control. It comes from knowing your worth and helping others realize theirs, too. She reminds us that sweetness is not a sign of weakness, and that caring deeply is a mark of strength.

A Living River: How You Can Walk with Oshun

Oshun's energy is always flowing. You don't have to be perfect or have special training to begin connecting with her. What she asks for most is honesty, openness, and love. If you feel drawn to her, you can begin a relationship in your own way, with respect and sincerity.

Here are a few gentle ways to welcome Oshun into your life:

- **Speak to her from the heart.** Whether in prayer, writing, or thought, let her know you are open to her guidance.
- **Offer her beauty.** A bowl of honey, fresh flowers, or a yellow candle can be a simple and powerful offering.
- **Spend time by the water.** Visit a river, lake, or even your bathtub. Talk to the water. Listen. Let it hold your emotions.
- **Celebrate joy.** Dance, laugh, wear bright colors, and find joy in life. Oshun shines when you do.
- **Practice kindness.** Be gentle with yourself and others. Share love freely, and let compassion lead your choices.

Most of all, remember that Oshun is not far away. She is within you. Her energy lives in every act of care, every moment of joy, and every time you choose beauty over bitterness.

Flowing Forward with Oshun

Oshun is a goddess of sweetness, but she is also a river of power. She has shaped cultures, healed hearts, inspired art, and stood firm against injustice. She is not just a symbol, she is a living presence, a spiritual force who continues to guide, nurture, and protect those who walk with her.

As we look to the future, Oshun offers us a path of balance. A path where justice and love are not opposites, but partners. A path where softness and strength can live together. A path where joy is not a reward, but a right.

To walk with Oshun is to walk in beauty. To flow with her is to trust that, even when life bends and twists like a river, you are being led somewhere sacred. Her golden energy shines through the challenges of our time, reminding us that healing is possible, love is powerful, and the divine feminine is rising.

No matter who you are or where you come from, Oshun's wisdom can touch your life. Her teachings can help you become more rooted, more open, more alive. And as you grow, you help her legacy grow too, carrying her light into the world, like sunlight dancing on the water.

CONCLUSION
EMBRACING THE SWEET
WATERS OF OSHUN

Throughout this book, you've been invited to walk along the flowing path of Oshun, the Orisha of rivers, love, beauty, and abundance. You've learned her stories, heard the voices of her devotees, and discovered the many ways she touches lives around the world. Now, as this journey comes to a close, a new beginning opens. The lessons of Oshun don't end on the page. They live on in you.

To embrace the sweet waters of Oshun is to welcome her energy into your life in simple, yet powerful ways. It means living with intention, treating yourself with care, and offering kindness to others. It means allowing joy to return, even after sorrow has passed. It means choosing beauty, not for attention, but as a celebration of life.

Let's pause for a moment and reflect on all she has offered us.

Oshun's Gifts: What She Teaches Us

Oshun teaches us that love is more than just emotion; it is a powerful force for healing, growth, and connection. Whether she appears in a gentle breeze by the water or in a moment of quiet courage, she reminds us that we are never alone. Her energy is always present, guiding us to stay true to ourselves and to walk with grace.

She offers many gifts:

- **Compassion** reminds us to be soft with ourselves and others.
- **Courage** helps us to stand firm when life is unfair.
- **Joy** encourages us to laugh, dance, and savor the sweetness of being alive.
- **Abundance**, showing us that prosperity begins in the heart before it reaches the hands.
- **Wisdom** leads us to trust our intuition and learn from our experiences.

She does not force or demand. She invites. She flows. She whispers. Through the quiet lessons of water and the beauty of golden light, Oshun helps us remember who we are.

Building a Deeper Connection

If you feel a strong bond with Oshun, that is no accident. She is known to choose those who need her most. Maybe you have gone through heartbreak. Perhaps you have felt lost and unsure of your purpose. Maybe you've always carried a light inside you that others didn't understand.

Oshun sees that light. She helps it grow.

Building a deeper relationship with her doesn't require fancy rituals or perfect words. What it does require is consistency, openness, and respect. You can begin right where you are. Here are a few ways to strengthen your connection:

- **Talk to her regularly.** Speak out loud, or in your heart. Share your dreams, fears, and hopes with her.
- **Create a sacred space.** This could be an altar, a shelf with her colors, or a corner by your bed where you place a flower or a bowl of water.
- **Celebrate life.** Eat sweet foods with joy. Dress in bright colors. Surround yourself with things that lift your spirit.
- **Practice gratitude.** Say thank you often. To her. To yourself. To life.
- **Follow her values.** Be generous. Be loving. Protect your peace. Move with elegance and strength.

Oshun is not just worshipped in temples or by rivers. She lives in everyday acts of beauty, care, and love. The more you honor her, the more you begin to embody her.

A Life of Flow

To live in flow means to stop resisting what your heart already knows. It means to trust that life, like a river, may bend and twist, but will carry you where you need to go. Flow is not about having no problems. It's about learning how to move through life with balance and grace.

Oshun teaches that softness is not a sign of weakness. It is wisdom. When you let go of what no longer serves you, you make room for what will. When you stop fighting your feelings, you begin to heal. When you trust your inner rhythm, you begin to shine.

In a world that often moves too fast and demands too much, Oshun gives you permission to slow down and reconnect. She asks you to listen to your body, to dance even when no one is watching, to laugh even when life feels heavy.

Living in flow also means being flexible. Rivers change their path when they need to. Sometimes they rise, sometimes they rest. Oshun reminds us to adjust without losing our essence. You are allowed to grow. You are allowed to shift. And you are allowed to protect your peace as you do.

Bringing Oshun into the World

Oshun's energy is not meant to be kept only in private rituals or quiet prayers. It is meant to flow into the world. When you live with love, share beauty, and help others heal, you become a vessel for her light.

Ask yourself:

- How can I bring more sweetness into my community?
- How can I stand up for justice while staying true to compassion?
- How can I honor the divine feminine in myself and others?

The world needs Oshun's energy now more than ever. We need rivers of care to wash away cruelty. We need golden light to remind us that beauty still exists. We need people like you, who choose to walk gently, but with purpose.

You may not realize it, but your journey with Oshun can inspire others. When you speak her name with respect, share her stories, and live by her values, you help keep her presence alive across generations.

Honoring Her in Your Own Way

There is no one right way to walk with Oshun. Her love is wide, her path is open, and she welcomes those who come with a pure heart. You do not need to know everything. You just need to begin with honesty.

Some people will feel called to study traditional practices. Others may light a candle, say a prayer, and go about their day with more awareness. Both paths are sacred when walked with care and respect.

What matters most is that your connection to her is real. Let it grow slowly, like a river flowing deeper over time. Be patient with yourself. You are not expected to be perfect. You are simply asked to be present.

And when you forget? When life feels heavy and the sweetness seems far away? Return to water. Return to stillness. Return to your breath. Oshun is never far. She waits by the river, ready to remind you of your worth.

Your River Continues

As you close this book, know that the journey is not ending, it is only just beginning. Oshun's river continues to flow through your life, offering guidance, peace, and beauty wherever you let her in.

You are not alone on this path. Around the world, people are walking with her. Some are dancing. Some are praying. Some are healing. And now, you are part of that beautiful current.

Let your life become a reflection of Oshun's energy. Be the person who brings joy into a room. Be the one who chooses softness over anger. Be the one who remembers the value of a kind word, a warm smile, a generous heart.

You are the river now.

Let your flow be sacred.

Let your love be strong.

Let your journey be golden.

Ase.

Next in Series

Discover the divine calm and power of Obatala, the Orisha of wisdom, justice, and peace. In Obatala: Guardian of Truth, Justice, and Divine Vision, explore sacred rituals, altar-building practices, and leadership lessons rooted in Yoruba spirituality.

Learn how Obatala shaped the world and how his teachings can shape yours.

Walk the white path of grace.

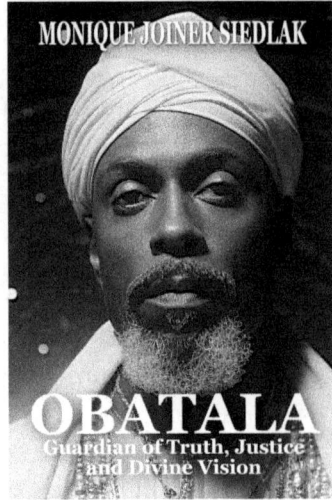

mojosiedlak.com/obatala

Bibliography

Barnet, M., & González, C. (1997). *Afro-Cuban religions*. Markus Wiener Publishers.

Bascom, W. (1969). *Ifa divination: Communication between gods and men in West Africa*. Indiana University Press.

Bynum, E. B. (2012). *The African unconscious: Roots of ancient mysticism and modern psychology* (2nd ed.). Cosimo Classics.

Clark, M. (2005). *Santería: Correcting the myths and uncovering the realities of a growing religion*. Praeger.

Conner, R. P., & Sparks, D. H. (2004). *Queering creole spiritual traditions: Lesbian, gay, bisexual, and transgender participation in African-inspired traditions in the Americas*. Routledge.

De La Torre, M. A. (2004). *Santería: The beliefs and rituals of a growing religion in America*. Wm. B. Eerdmans Publishing.

Drewal, H. J., & Mason, J. (1998). *Beads, body, and soul: Art and light in the Yoruba universe*. UCLA Fowler Museum of Cultural History.

Falola, T., & Genova, A. (2006). *Yoruba traditions and African American religious nationalism*. University Press of Florida.

Fanon, F. (2008). *Black skin, white masks* (R. Philcox, Trans.). Grove Press. (Original work published 1952)

Fernandez Olmos, M., & Paravisini-Gebert, L. (2011). *Creole religions of the Caribbean: An introduction from Vodou and Santería to Obeah and Espiritismo* (2nd ed.). NYU Press.

Gonzalez-Wippler, M. (2002). *Santería: The religion: Faith, rites, magic*. Llewellyn Publications.

Hall, G. M. (2005). *Slavery and African ethnicities in the Americas: Restoring the links*. University of North Carolina Press.

Hayes, K. E. (2011). *Holy harlots: Femininity, sexuality, and black magic in film and literature*. University of California Press.

Hucks, T. E. (2012). *Yoruba traditions and African American religious nationalism*. University Press of Florida.

Johnson, S. (2001). *The history of the Yorubas: From the earliest times to the beginning of the British Protectorate*. CSS Press. (Original work published 1921)

King, R. (1999). *African American religion and the civil rights movement in Arkansas*. University Press of Mississippi.

Long, C. H. (2001). *Significations: Signs, symbols, and images in the interpretation of religion*. Fortress Press.

Lugo, A. (2011). *Fragmented lives, assembled parts: Culture, capitalism, and conquest at the U.S.-Mexico border*. University of Texas Press.

Bibliography

Murphy, J. M. (1994). *Working the spirit: Ceremonies of the African diaspora*. Beacon Press.

Otero, S. (2010). *Yemayá y Ochún: Motherhood, syncretism, and identity in the Afro-Cuban diaspora*. SUNY Press.

Pinn, A. B. (2003). *Terror and triumph: The nature of Black religion*. Fortress Press.

Shell, M. (2013). *Children of the earth spirit: The healing journey of an Afro-Indigenous woman*. Indigenous Voices Press.

Sweet, J. H. (2003). *Recreating Africa: Culture, kinship, and religion in the African-Portuguese world, 1441–1770*. University of North Carolina Press.

Thompson, R. F. (1984). *Flash of the spirit: African and Afro-American art and philosophy*. Vintage Books.

Womack, Y. (2013). *Afrofuturism: The world of Black sci-fi and fantasy culture*. Lawrence Hill Books.

WANT TO BE FIRST TO KNOW?!

SIGN UP FOR MY NEWSLETTER TO RECEIVE NEW RELEASE UPDATES & SPECIALS!

mojosiedlak.com/newsletter-signup

Also By The Author

African Spirituality Beliefs and Practices

Hoodoo

Seven African Powers: The Orishas

Cooking for the Orishas

Lucumi: The Ways of Santeria

Voodoo of Louisiana

Haitian Vodou

Orishas of Trinidad

Connecting with your Ancestors

Blood Magick

The Orishas

Vodun: West Africa's Spiritual Life

Marie Laveau: Life of a Voodoo Queen

Candomblé: Dancing for the God

Umbanda

Exploring the Rich and Diverse World of African Spirituality

African Shamanism: The Power of Spiritual Healing and Transformation

About the Author

Monique Joiner Siedlak is a writer, witch, and warrior on a mission to awaken people to their greatest potential through the power of storytelling infused with mysticism, modern paganism, and new age spirituality. At the young age of 12, she began rigorously studying the fascinating philosophy of Wicca. By the time she was 20, she was self-initiated into the craft, and hasn't looked back ever since. To this day, she has authored over 50 books pertaining to the magick and mysteries of life.

To find out more about Monique Joiner Siedlak artistically, spiritually, and personally, feel free to visit her **official website**.

www.mojosiedlak.com

facebook.com/mojosiedlak

x.com/mojosiedlak

instagram.com/mojosiedlak

pinterest.com/mojosiedlak

youtube.com/@MoniqueJoinerSiedlak_Author

bookbub.com/authors/monique-joiner-siedlak